THE CATHOLIC UNIVERSITY OF AMERICA
CANON LAW STUDIES
Number 74

THE DIOCESAN SYNOD

AN HISTORICAL CONSPECTUS AND COMMENTARY

A DISSERTATION

Submitted to the Faculty of Canon Law of the Catholic University of America in Partial Fulfillment of the Requirements for the Degree of

DOCTORATE OF CANON LAW

BY

FRANCIS BERNARD DONNELLY, A.M., S.T.L., J.C.L.,
Priest of the Diocese of Brooklyn

THE CATHOLIC UNIVERSITY OF AMERICA
WASHINGTON, D. C.
1932

Nihil Obstat:

VALENTINUS T. SCHAAF, O.F.M., J.C.D.,
Censor Deputatus.
Washingtonii, D. C., die XXII Aprilis, 1932.

Imprimatur:

THOMAS EDMUNDUS MOLLOY, D.D.,
Episcopus Brooklyniensis.
Brooklynii, die XXII Aprilis, 1932.

Printed by
THE PAULIST PRESS
New York, N. Y.

TABLE OF CONTENTS

PAGE

FOREWORD vii

PART I

EVOLUTION OF THE PRESENT DISCIPLINE

CHAPTER I

NATURE OF THE DIOCESAN SYNOD 1

Art. I. Synod in General 1

Art. II. The Diocesan Synod 2

Art. III. Other Legislative Assemblies 4

CHAPTER II

ORIGIN AND EARLY DEVELOPMENT OF THE DIOCESAN SYNOD 7

Art. I. The Presbyterium 8

Art. II. Origin of the Diocesan Synod 10

Appendix: Ecclesiastical Roman Law 14

Art. III. The Early Legislation on the Diocesan Synod 15

CHAPTER III

GENERAL LEGISLATION ON THE DIOCESAN SYNOD 19

Art. I. Ante-Tridentine Legislation 19

Art. II. Tridentine Legislation 22

Art. III. Post-Tridentine Regulations 24

Art. IV. Juridical Aspect of the Non-observance of the Tridentine Law 28

Résumé 34

PART II
LEGISLATION OF THE CODE

CHAPTER IV

PAGE

THE CONVOCATION OF THE SYNOD 37

Art. I. Obligation of the Synod 37
1. In Each Diocese 37
2. In Dioceses Subject to the Same Bishop 38
3. In an Abbey or Prelature *Nullius* 41
4. In a Vicariate Apostolic 42

Art. II. Right of Convocation 43
1. The Residential Bishop 44
2. Abbot or Prelate *Nullius* 46
3. Vicars and Prefects Apostolic 47
4. Administrators Apostolic 48
5. Coadjutor Bishop 49
6. Pro-Vicars and Pro-Prefects Apostolic 49
7. Vicar General 50
8. Vicar Capitular or Administrator 51

Art. III. Frequency of the Synod 52

Art. IV. Place of the Synod 54

CHAPTER V

MEMBERSHIP OF THE SYNOD 56

Art. I. Prescribed Membership 57
1. Vicar General 58
2. Cathedral Chapter or Board of Consultors 59
3. Rector of the Major Seminary 60
4. Vicars Forane 62
5. Representatives of the Collegiate Chapters 62
6. The Pastoral Clergy 63
7. Religious Superiors 68

Art. II. Invited Members 70

Art. III. Obligation of Attendance 73
1. The Obligated Members 73
2. Legitimate Absence 75
3. Punishment of Absentees 76

CHAPTER VI

PAGE

PREPARATION OF THE SYNOD 77
ART. I. PRE-SYNODAL COMMISSIONS 78
1. Appointment 78
2. Work of the Commissions 80
ART. II. APPOINTMENT OF SYNODAL OFFICIALS 81
ART. III. PREPARATORY SESSIONS 84

CHAPTER VII

SYNODAL LEGISLATION 87
ART. I. OBJECT OF THE SYNODAL STATUTES 87
1. Extent of the Synodal Statutes 88
2. Limitations of the Statutes 92
ART. II. SPECIAL TYPES OF SYNODAL LAWS 95
1. Invalidating and Inhabilitating Laws 95
2. Personal Laws 96
3. Laws for Peregrini 97
4. Laws for Orientals 100

CHAPTER VIII

CELEBRATION OF THE SYNOD 102
ART. I. ORDER OF PRECEDENCE IN THE SYNOD 104
ART. II. PROFESSION OF FAITH 108
ART. III. ENACTMENT OF THE SYNODAL LEGISLATION 110
1. The Legislator of the Synod 110
2. Promulgation of the Legislation 113
3. Obligation and Force of the Synodal Statutes 114
ART. IV. APPROBATION OF OFFICIALS IN THE SYNOD 115
1. Synodal Examiners 115
2. Parish Priest Consultors 117
3. Synodal Judges 118
APPENDIX 119
BIBLIOGRAPHY 125

FOREWORD

ALTHOUGH the Church states unequivocally that bishops as successors of the Apostles and divinely instituted rulers of particular churches have the legislative power in their dioceses, it has provided that the ordinary way in which this jurisdiction should be exercised is in the legislative assembly of a diocesan synod. This provision, of course, does not destroy the right of a bishop to enact outside the synod whatever special regulations are suddenly made necessary. For even in the synod it is only the bishop who actually gives legal force to its enactments, and therefore as the sole legislator of the diocese his powers should not be so curtailed. But the experience of the Church throughout the centuries has proved that the wise course is that a bishop gather his clergy about him at stated times to discuss with them the conditions and needs of the diocese and decide on the necessary regulations. The regular continuance of this practice, therefore, has been provided for in several canons of the Code, and it is a consideration of these which is to be the subject of this study.

This dissertation is principally a commentary on the present legislation. Its purpose is to explain the present law of the Church concerning the preparation for and celebration of the diocesan synod. But in doing this it is not right to deprive this consideration of the existing law of its background by ignoring entirely its origin and evolution to its present form. Therefore, an attempt has been made to indicate the principal stages of the history of the legislation on the synod. This historical summary is not intended to be a work of original research, as both the lack of sources and shortness of time allotted for this study make such an objective impossible. It is given only in order that the purpose and explanation of the present legislation may be seen in its proper setting; for it is only in this way that the diocesan synod may be understood as the Church intends it to be regarded.

The writer wishes to acknowledge the use of an unprinted dissertation on the synod by the Most Rev. J. C. McGuigan. He also takes this occasion to express his gratitude to the Faculty of Canon Law of the University and to Rev. Dr. John J. Carberry for their very kind assistance.

PART I

EVOLUTION OF THE PRESENT DISCIPLINE

CHAPTER I

NATURE OF THE DIOCESAN SYNOD

ARTICLE I. SYNOD IN GENERAL

THE word *synod* is of Greek origin, being a transliteration of the word σύνοδος (*meeting*). According to etymologists[1] it is a compound of the preposition σὺν (*with*) and ὁδὸς (*road*). Apparently this word was first used in a figurative sense. For a meeting of any group would take place because of common interests, that is, because figuratively those present were traveling on the same road and were striving for the same destination. At any rate the idea of a fellow-traveler suggests a special, intimate relation.

Even in pre-Christian times the word *synod* had its present meaning of *meeting* or *assembly*. Plato, Herodotus, and Thucydides used it in this sense to designate different types of gatherings,[2] and it even received a Latinized form with the same meaning.[3] Therefore it is not surprising that, in addition to the word *concilium* which Tertullian[4] appears to have introduced in the West, this word in both its Greek and Latin forms was very properly used to designate the various Christian gatherings in which ecclesiastical matters were discussed.[5] For a long time the words *synod* and *council* continued to be used interchangeably by ecclesiastical writers to designate any of the various Church gatherings.[6] But by the seventeenth century, according to the testimony of Doujat,[7] the word *synod* was

[1] Cf. Liddell-Scott, *Greek-English Lexicon.*

[2] Cf. Liddell-Scott, *Greek-English Lexicon, v.* σύνοδος; Pickering, *Lexicon of the Greek Language,* v. σύνοδος.

[3] Cf. *Lexicon totius Latinitatis Aegidii Forcellini,* IV, 645.

[4] *De Jejuniis,* c. 13—*M. P. L.,* II, 972.

[5] *Canones Apostolorum,* c. 36—Mansi, I, 35.

[6] Cf. Benedict XIV, *De Synodo Dioecesana* 1. I, c. 1, n. 1; Wernz-Vidal, *De Personis,* p. 664, n. 1.

[7] *Praenotiones Canonicae,* 1. II, c. 1, n. 6 as referred to by Phillips, *Die Diöcesansynode,* p. 19.

used to designate the diocesan synod alone,[8] and Bellarmine[9] insisted that the name *council* could not be properly given to the diocesan synod. From that time on and even in the present Code the word *synod* has been used almost always to refer to the diocesan synod.[10]

Article II. The Diocesan Synod

The diocesan synod may be defined as a legitimate assembly of a representative body of the clergy of a diocese who have been convoked by the bishop for the purpose of discussing and adopting whatever measures are necessary or useful for the welfare of the diocese.[11] As it stands this definition is comprised of three elements. In order to clarify them further it will be well to consider each briefly.

The first requirement for a diocesan synod is that it be an assembly of the clergy of a diocese. But in addition to that, it must be conducted according to the requirements of the legislation in the Code. In that sense it should be legitimate, so as to distinguish it from other clerical gatherings, such as clerical conferences or even pro-synodal meetings.[12] According to canon 358, however only a representation of the clergy need be summoned by the bishop, though he may call as many of the others as he believes the needs of the diocese can spare. The purpose of this provision is to obviate the difficulty which many bishops formerly experienced in the convocation of the synod. Finally, the clergy who are to be members

[8] However, the term *sancta synodus* is often used as an appellation for the ecumenical council. Cf. Benedict XIV, *De Synodo Dioecesana,* 1. I, c. 3, n. 1.

[9] *De Conciliis,* I, 4.

[10] In previous centuries the synod has had other names; viz. *concilium episcopale* or *episcopi, synodus episcopalis, capitulum, capitulum synodale, concilium synodale, synodalis congregatio, concilium civile, generale presbyterorum concilium, generalis sacerdotum synodus, universalis synodus, publica* or *plenaria* or *plena synodus.* Cf. Phillips, *Die Diöcesansynode,* pp. 8-9; Oesterle, *Praelectiones Juris Canonici,* I, 179.

[11] Canons 356-358.

[12] Pro-synodal meetings were to be called in certain places whenever it was impossible to hold the synod. Cf. Benedict XIV, *De Synodo Dioecesana,* 1. I, c. 2, n. 5; Claeys-Bouuaert, *De Canonica Cleri Saecularis Obedientia,* p. 86 ff.

of the synod must be from the diocese, although they will not all be secular priests. Since the matters which are to be treated at the synod should be only those which concern the diocese and since the synodal legislation will oblige only the diocese, it follows that only when their assistance is needed to conduct the synod properly will extra-diocesan priests have reason to be present and even then they may not be given a vote in the proceedings.

Convocation by the bishop is the second essential for the synod. As the head of the diocese, the bishop alone has the right to convoke the synod. He may exercise this act of jurisdiction himself or delegate another. But unless he is its author, the synod is convoked illegitimately. The Code [13] even explicitly states that the Vicar General, without a special mandate, and the Vicar Capitular have not this power. The obligation of holding the synod rests, therefore, upon the bishop. He must see to it that it is celebrated at the proper time and according to the norms stated in the Code and in the liturgical books.

The purpose of the synod constitutes the third and final element of the definition. This is stated in canon 356 §1. Since the bishop alone in the diocese has the power to make laws, it is clear that he need not convoke the synod to legislate for the diocese. The purpose of the synod, therefore, can only be to enact laws after consulting the clergy about the needs of the diocese.[14] Such a procedure gives hope of more fruitful legislation. For not only will the needs of the diocese be better known, but the clergy after consultative sessions on the various matters will be more impressed with their importance, and therefore more apt to see to their observance.[15] The matters to be considered are only those which affect the welfare of the diocese. Both the discussion and legislation should relate only to these. The synod is not competent on affairs outside the diocese, nor should it attempt to legislate on such matters. Finally, of course, its regulations on diocesan matters should always be confined to the limitations prescribed by the common law.

[13] C. 357 §1.

[14] However, the clergy have a decisive vote in the approbation of some officials. Cf. cc. 385-388, 1574.

[15] Cf. Benedict XIV, *De Synodo Dioecesana*, 1. I, c. 2.

Article III. Other Legislative Assemblies

Besides the diocesan synod, the Code [16] prescribes several other legislative assemblies; namely, the ecumenical council, the plenary council, the provincial council, and the conference of bishops.[17] A brief consideration of each will show how they differ from the synod.

Ecumenical Council. This is a gathering of bishops of the entire Church and other prelates designated by the Code, convoked by the Pope alone, who either personally or through a legate presides over the assembly and supervises its actions. The purpose of the ecumenical council is to define certain matters of faith or ordain points of common discipline. Of its nature this is the supreme legislative body in the Church, but only when the Pope is at its head. As a rule all the prelates who are called to the council have a deliberative vote, but their decision is of no value unless the Pope approves what has been done.[18] Once the decrees have been approved, however, and promulgated by the Pope, they oblige the entire Church.

Plenary Council. Following the text of canon 281 this may be defined as an assembly of the Ordinaries of several provinces after they have obtained the permission of the Pope and been called together by his legate, who will preside over the council. No longer, therefore, is a plenary council synonymous with a national council.[19] For a plenary council might be a meeting of the Ordinaries of provinces in more than one country, or it might have as its members the Ordinaries of only some of the provinces in a country. The frequency of this gathering is not determined by the Code; its celebration, then, should depend on the needs of the provinces. The fathers of the council are to decide what matters will be discussed, but of course the council is competent only about what concerns

[16] Cc. 222-229, 281-292.

[17] In the past there have been types of ecclesiastical gatherings the best known of which is the mixed synod. Cf. Hefele-Clark, *History of Church Councils*, I, 3-6; Phillips, *Die Diöcesansynode*, pp. 10-12.

[18] Can. 223 §3 states that theologians and canonists, who may be invited, have only a consultative vote.

[19] Cf. Hefele-Clark, *History of Church Councils*, I, 5.

the provinces that are represented. In the framing of any legislation the prelates mentioned in canon 282 have a deliberative vote; any other clerics have only a consultative vote. Whatever is enacted ought not to be promulgated until it has been submitted to the Sacred Congregation of the Council for approval. Once permission has been given for the publication of this legislation and it has been promulgated according to the manner decided upon in the council, it has the force of law from which, according to canon 292 §2, even the Ordinaries themselves cannot dispense unless for a grave reason in a particular case.

PROVINCIAL COUNCIL. This is an assembly of the metropolitan and the suffragan bishops of a province, which is to be held every twenty years [20] in order to provide for the needs of the entire province. Except for a limited membership [21] and its consequent restricted competence, the norms for the celebration of the provincial council are practically the same as for the plenary council.

CONFERENCE OF BISHOPS. Somewhat similar to the provincial council is the prescribed conference of bishops. For the first time this has been imposed by general law.[22] As its name designates, it is made up principally of bishops; but all *Ordinarii locorum* have the right to be present.[23] Usually these will be all from the same province, though in exceptional cases archbishops who have no suffragans, and bishops and abbots or prelates *nullius* who are not subject to a metropolitan see, will attend the conference of the province in which they assist at the provincial council.[24] The conference of bishops is

[20] C. 283.

[21] The Code gives to some who do not have to be invited to the plenary council the right to be present at the provincial council. Canon 286 §3 states that the members of the cathedral chapters, or the diocesan consultors, are to be invited and to designate two of their number to represent them at the council. The major superiors of clerical exempt religious and the superiors of monastic congregations are also given the right to be invited. In both instances, however, only a consultative vote is given.

[22] Before the Code the holding of these conferences was only the practice in several sections of the Church, although the Holy See on several occasions strongly recommended its adoption in other places. Cf. Wernz-Vidal, *De Personis,* pp. 579-580.

[23] Cc. 292 §1, 198.

[24] Cc. 292 §2, 285.

to be summoned at least every five years by the metropolitan or the senior suffragan to meet at the place determined at the last conference. There steps are to be taken to attend to the needs of the different dioceses as well as to prepare the matters to be treated in the next provincial council. In this way, unless the Holy See provides otherwise, the cause of religion in these places can be better safeguarded during the long interim of twenty years between provincial councils.

CHAPTER II

ORIGIN AND EARLY DEVELOPMENT OF THE DIOCESAN SYNOD

A STUDY of the early organization of the Church reveals that the holding of assemblies similar to the present provincial councils was a frequent practice.[1] In some places the gatherings were the means used to meet the need the daughter churches had of the nourishment of counsel and assistance from the mother church; while in other sections this practice arose as a means of uniting neighboring churches against the hostile conditions and adverse influences of the times.[2] Even as early as the end of the second century Tertullian [3] wrote of this practice existing in the East; and apparently it spread to the West soon after this. For from the fourth century on many councils in both the East and West prescribed the regular celebration of these gatherings. Bishops were obliged to attend the councils in their own province; and in the event that they could not attend a legate was to be sent in their stead.[4] Those who violated these prescriptions were threatened with serious penalties.[5] Experience had taught even at that early date that the advantages these gatherings offered were not to be disregarded.

There is not, however, similar early evidence for the existence of the diocesan synod. Of course, it may be that meetings similar to

[1] Hatch, *Organization of the Early Christian Church,* p. 170 ff.

[2] Bingham, *Origines Ecclesiasticae,* I, 193 ff.; V, 417-430; Hatch, *Organization of the Early Christian Church,* p. 174 ff.; Schaff, *History of the Christian Church,* II, 176-178; Alzog, *Manual of Church History,* 1, 405-409.

[3] *De Jejuniis,* c. 13—*M. P. L.,* II, 972.

[4] Council of Laodicea (320), c. 40—Mansi, II, 48; Council of Nicea (325), c. 5—Mansi, II, 670; Council of Antioch (340), c. 20—Mansi, II, 1315; 3 Council of Carthage (398), c. 2—Mansi, III, 880; 4 Council of Chalcedon (451), 2. 20—Mansi, VI, 1165; 2 Council of Arles (452), c. 18—Mansi, VII, 880.

[5] 2 Council of Arles (452), c. 19—Mansi, VII, 880; Council of Agde (506), c. 30—Mansi, VIII, 330.

it were held in some places concurrently.[6] But any legislation prescribing it is of a later date. There are, however, some indications of its beginnings which may be considered before the early legislation is examined.

Article I. The Presbyterium

The organization of the diocese,[7] as it now exists, is the product of an evolution, the hands of time and circumstance having molded it into its present form. In the beginning there was not, of course, the complex organization that now exists but a very simple unit that alone was necessary. But just what the exact make-up was in all places has long been disputed. Inability to understand exactly the language of the known evidence is a real bar to any definite conclusions even among Catholic writers.

There is, however, a unity of opinion among all on the existence in practically all the churches of a body made up of the clergy, and known as the *presbyterium,* to which the government was entrusted.[8] This mode of administration was introduced, perhaps in imitation of a similar Jewish governing body, the *synedrion,* by the Apostles and their missionary associates, who, when they had to leave their newly established communities, gave the government to a group of the clergy. The question of its definite organization offers some difficulty. The letters of Ignatius of Antioch[9] make it evident that

[6] Thomassinus, *Vetus et Nova Disciplina de Beneficiis,* p. II, l. 3, c. 73, n. 1; Benedict XIV, *De Synodo Dioecesana,* l. 1, c. 1, n. 6-7.

[7] Originally this name *diocese* belonged to the divisions of the Roman Empire made by Diocletian, and included in its confines several distinct churches under bishops. (Cf. Council of Nicea (321), c. 5—Mansi, II, 670; 2 Council of Constantinople (381), c. 2—Mansi, III, 559.) However, it was also used in its present ecclesiastical sense in several places (3 Council of Carthage (398), c. 42, 46—Mansi, III, 887-90), and later gradually replaced the previous appellations *church* and *parish.* Cf. Van Hove, "Diocese," *Catholic Encyclopedia,* V, 1; Fourneret, "Diocèse," *Dictionnaire de Théologie Catholique,* IV, 1362-1363.

[8] Duchesne, *Early History of the Christian Church,* pp. 62-70; Michiels, *De Origine Episcopatus,* pp. 277-286, 364, 367-68, 373, 414; Moran, *Government of the Church in the First Century,* pp. 72-95.

[9] Ep. ad Ephes., IV—*M. P. G.*, V, 647; Ep. ad Trall., VII—*M. P. G.*, V, 679; Ep. ad Philad., IV, VII—*M. P. G.*, V, 699, 702; Ep. ad Smyrn., VIII—*M. P. G.*, V, 714; Ep. ad Polycarp., VI—*M. P. G.*, V, 725.

throughout Asia Minor and Syria [10] the bishop was the supreme authority. Schaff [11] and others may regard these texts as later interpolations, but as Lightfoot [12] shows whether the Greek or Syriac texts of the letters are accepted as the original version the testimony of both is convincing and the fear of a later interpolation unfounded. In the other sections of the Church the supremacy of the bishop is not so evident. But at least there is nothing to make a monarchical episcopate impossible. For, besides the existence of a bishop in Jerusalem from the beginning, the fact that when the monarchical episcopate is known to have been accepted by all it was not regarded as a new institution and left no record of any protest would seem to indicate that it had always existed as such. That appears to be a reasonable deduction.

The very nature and purpose of the *presbyterium* as a means of church government implies that it must have had legislative powers to do its work. That would be among its most important functions. Thus it is that Ignatius called it an *apostolic senate,*[13] a *senate of of God,* and a *council of apostles.*[14] It is spoken of as existing in a similar way at Carthage by Cyprian,[15] at Rome by Pope Cornelius,[16] and at Antioch by Epiphanius.[17] In a word, the work of the *presbyterium* appears to have been much the same as that of the present day cathedral chapter or board of consultors.[18] Accordingly, since all the clergy were members of this *presbyterium,* such a gathering as the diocesan synod was without purpose. Its work was already being done. Only when the *presbyterium* would not include in its membership the entire body of the clergy would its work have to

[10] Batiffol, *Études d'Histoire et de Théologie Positive,* pp. 229-231.

[11] *History of the Christian Church,* II, 144-148.

[12] *Dissertations on the Apostolic Age,* pp. 173-174, 198-200, 239-243.

[13] Ep. ad Magn., VI—*M. P. G.*, V, 667.

[14] Ep. ad Trall., III—*M. P. G.*, V, 678.

[15] Epist. VI—*M. P. L.*, IV, 248; Epist. X—*M. P. L.*, IV, 253; Epist. XXIV —*M. P. L.,* IV, 287.

[16] Epist. V—Mansi, I, 831.

[17] *Adversus Haereses* LVII, 1—*M. P. G.*, XLI, 994.

[18] Bouix, in his *Tractatus de Capitulis,* p. 5 ff., maintains that the *presbyterium* gave rise to the cathedral chapter.

be supplemented by that of the synod. Such would be the case when the Church would spread itself more in the outlying districts and cease to be confined almost entirely to the cities and towns where it had arisen.

Article II. Origin of the Diocesan Synod

When in the fourth century the Church ceased to be persecuted and in addition received legal recognition, it was offered a remarkable opportunity for advancement. Previously there had been many obstacles in its way. Now very many of these were removed and its work could go ahead. So there is found a very notable progress in the work of the Church.[19] Not only was the faith solidified in the urban centers where it had taken hold in the beginning, but it became more firm in the rural districts. The numbers of the faithful outside the cities and towns so increased that it was necessary to make provisions for their care by a distinct rural clergy.[20] These were to be in charge of newly established churches and were to reside permanently in their respective districts.

It was this development that apparently gave rise to the synod. For, since some of the clergy had to live at a distance from the city or town where the *presbyterium* would meet, they could not participate in its regular activities. It is likely that in order to supply for this means of obtaining their counsel and of informing them of the regular provincial decrees the rural clergy would be called together on certain occasions whenever the needs of their work permitted. This would not mean the abolition of the *presbyterium*. That was to continue as before.[21] But the well-being of the Church demanded that its work be completed by some means taken to provide occasional consultations with the rural clergy.

[19] Alzog, *Manual of Church History*, I, 499-505; Schaff, *History of the Christian Church*, III, 11-13, 67 ff.; Fisher, *History of the Christian Church*, p. 81 ff.; Milman, *History of Christianity*, p. 296.

[20] Coady, *Appointment of Pastors*, pp. 7-13; Bastnagel, *Appointment of Parochial Adjutants and Assistants*, pp. 4-11; Cunningham, *Historical Background of National Parishes*, p. 3 ff.

[21] Cf. Jerome, *Comment. in Isaiam Prophetam*, 1. II, c. 3—*M. P. L.*, XXIV, 61.

Though this change would furnish the occasion, one is forced to admit the lack of certainty about any of the details concerning the origin of the synod. The available evidence consists principally in accounts, some of which are very summary, of meetings held under the supervision of a bishop. Even in regard to these authors disagree as to which were really diocesan. In other words, one comes upon the existence of the synod without being able to give a complete or even satisfactory account of its origin. An attempt may be made, however, to point out some of the probabilities in this connection.

The first diocesan synod is said to have been held in the East. Authors [22] generally accept as the first of these the synod of Alexandria [23] held in 321. However it must be noted that, even though this assembly was under the supervision of the Bishop of Alexandria, it was attended by priests and deacons of the Mareotic region, and consequently it was not a strictly diocesan gathering. Likewise there is some reason to doubt the diocesan character of the Synod of Ptolemais (411) [24] because, from the accounts of its celebration, it would appear that there were other bishops present. As far as the extant summary records indicate,[25] it seems correct to conclude that a gathering at Jerusalem in 415 was strictly a diocesan meeting. However, even this cannot be said to establish definitely the origin of the synod in the East. For even if these assemblies were of a diocesan nature, the purpose apparently was different from that of the synod. The accounts of the gatherings seem to indicate that they were not convoked as the usual way to legislate for the diocese or even to promulgate provincial decrees, but as special means necessary to protect the clergy and the people against the various here-

[22] Hinschius, *System des Katholischen Kirchenrechts,* III, 583, note 5; Wernz, *Jus Decretalium,* II b, 731; Cocchi, *Commentarium in Codicem,* III, 240; Ayrinhac, *Constitution of the Church,* p. 194. Phillips does not consider the synod in the East.

[23] Mansi, II, 558; Hardouin, I, 310; Hefele-Clark, I, 248. Apparently Augustine (*Commentary on Canon Law,* II, 384, note 1) confuses this with a previous sectional gathering at Alexandria in saying that nearly a hundred bishops attended. Cf. Mansi, II, 554; Hardouin, I, 295; Hefele-Clark, I, 247.

[24] Mansi, IV, 1-6; Hardouin, I, 112; Hefele-Clark, II, 445.

[25] Mansi, IV, 307-312; Hefele-Clark, II, 449.

sies or some other serious danger. In other words, they appear to be an extraordinary means devised to meet abnormal conditions rather than one of the usual ways of administering the diocese. Perhaps this might explain why there is no record of any Oriental legislation on the synod and why it could be said that the Oriental Church adopted the synod, as now understood, from the Latin Church.[26] Therefore it is more likely that the early diocesan gatherings of the East were not really diocesan synods, principally because they were not legislative assemblies such as the synod has always been. It appears that one must look to the Church in the West for the origin of the synod.

The theory of Savagnone [27] in this question merits examination. This is based on the interpretation, though an incorrect one,[28] of the Theodosian Code made in the *Breviarium Alarici* which was the law for Romans in Visigothic Spain from 506 until 654.[29] Savagnone maintains that it is impossible to discover the origin of the synod within the Roman Empire, either in ecclesiastical Roman law or in ancient canon law. Therefore, on the strength of this passage of the *Breviarium,* he concludes that the synod originated in Spain. It was a consequence of the politico-religious crisis that arose after the conquest of the Visigoths because of the resulting decline of the previous wide authority of the metropolitan and the newly acquired autonomy of the bishop. And though it did not spread to any great extent during the three centuries after its rise, it received a

[26] Papp-Szilagyi, *Enchiridion Juris Ecclesiae Orientalis Catholicae,* pp. 23, 129.

[27] "Le origini del sinodo diocesano e l' 'Interpretatio' alla c. 23, Th. XVI, 2," *Studi in Onore di Biagio Brugi,* pp. 567-600.

[28] The text as found in the Theodosian Code (c. 23, XVI, 2) is: " . . . *et a suae dioeceseos synodis audiantur* . . ." According to Gothofredus (*Codex Theodosianus cum Perpetuis Commentariis,* Vol. 6, part 1, 57-62) reference is made to assemblies of the metropolitan and bishops from the territorial divisions of the Empire established by Diocletian and known as dioceses. He therefore concludes that the author of the *Breviarium* interpreted this passage wrongly when he wrote " . . . *convocatis ab episcopo dioecesanis presbyteris* . . " probably for the reason that, since only one bishop is spoken of, the word *dioecesanis* apparently cannot be interpreted in the sense it had in Roman Law.

[29] Cf. Ziegler, *Church and State in Visigothic Spain,* pp. 27, 59-60.

very marked impetus upon the publication of the peusdo-Isidorian decretals in the ninth century when the power of the metropolitan received an even greater setback.

It is outside the scope of this brief historical survey to examine Savagnone's theory in detail. Briefly, it may be said that in several instances the conclusions drawn do not appear to be justified by the evidence given. Thus the attempts of the author to disprove conclusively the diocesan character of the gatherings at Alexandria, Ptolemais, and Jerusalem already referred to are not as convincing as he would have them. Then, too, his theory that the strongly concentrated power of the metropolitan over the bishop would certainly make the synod impossible is far from substantiated by the evidence that is adduced.[30] The strongest argument for the theory is that it explains the sudden increase of legislation concerning the synod that was enacted in the councils of France and Germany from the seventh century on. De Wretschus [31] shows that, besides being the law for the territory that was under the control of the Visigoths, the *Breviarium* was also used in Germany and the other parts of France as an interpretation of Roman law. Apparently, too, it influenced ecclesiastical legislation. This might explain why insistence began to be laid in these territories on the celebration of the synod. Therefore, even if the synod did not originate in Spain, at least the growing practice of celebrating it received there strong stimulation.

One may certainly maintain that a diocesan synod was held at Auxerre in 578. The complete account that has been preserved is ample proof of this.[32] It is possible, however, that a synod was held in the West even earlier, either at Rome in 390,[33] or at Tournai

[30] Cf. Appendix of this article.

[31] De Usu Breviarii Alaricani Forensi et Scholastico per Hispaniam, Galliam, Italiam Regionesque Vicinos—*Theodosiani Libri XVI* (Kreuger-Mommsen edition), Vol. I, part 1, cccvii-ccclx. Cf. Gothofredus, *Codex Theodosianus cum Perpetuis Commentariis,* I, ccxxvi.

[32] Mansi, IX, 911-918; Hardouin, III, 443-448.

[33] Cf. Second Epistle of Pope Siricius—Mansi, III, 664; Hardouin, I, 852-853. However, since the purpose of this gathering was to condemn Jovinian, it is probable that this was an extraordinary event rather than an instance of the regular practice of the synod.

in 523,[34] or at Londaff in 560.[35] But the incompleteness of the extant accounts of these assemblies makes any conclusion doubtful.

Appendix: Ecclesiastical Roman Law

Although the sources of Roman law indicate the existence of the ecumenical council[36] and provincial council,[37] both of which are given the name *synod,* nothing has been found that could be taken as a reference to the diocesan synod as now understood. As a consequence Savagnone [38] concludes that such an institution was not known in the empire at that time.

He substantiates this conclusion by the fact that in two places in which regulations are made concerning the alienation of Church property there is required the deliberation of the clergy and the bishop of the city together with the metropolitan who will preside over the gathering; [39] and even in addition the presence of two bishops from the provincial council in order that the meeting may have a provincial character.[40] Certainly this would be a limitation on the power of the bishop. But the conclusion of Savagnone that it proves a strong metropolitan domination [41] which would make impossible the existence of the synod as later understood, is too far-reaching. It might very well be that such regulations, made in this instance of the alienation of property as special precautionary methods to prevent

[34] Mansi, VIII, 587.

[35] Mansi, IX, 763; Hardouin, III, 343; Hefele-Clark, IV, 380.

[36] 3, 3, C. I., 1, 1; 4, C. I., I, 1; 7, 12, C. I., I, 1; 7, 15, C. I., I, 1; 23, C. I., I, 3; 8, pr., C. I., I, 5; 8, 5, C. I., I, 5; Nov. 131, c. 1; Nov. 137, c. 1.

[37] 23, C. Th., XVI, 2; 16, C. I., I, 2; 29 pr., C. I., I, 4; 29, 11, C. I., I, 4; Nov. 11; Nov. 67, c. 4; Nov. 123, c. 3, 10, 22; Nov. 131, c. 3; Nov. 137, c. 1, 4, 6.

[38] "Le origini del sinodo diocesano et l' 'Interpretatio' alla c. 23, Th., XVI, 2," *Studi in Onore di Biagio Brugi,* pp. 575-79; *Annali del Seminario Giuridico della R. Universita di Palermo,* pp. 4, 146.

[39] Nov. 46, c. 1.

[40] Nov. 67, c. 4.

[41] ". . . *Ci prova altresì come repugnasse al forte accentramento metropolitico l'autonomia vescovile, di cui il sinodo diocesano e l'indice piu caratteristico*"—*Studi in Onore di Biagio Brugi,* p. 577.

likely abuses, were therefore exceptional and would not prove that such a mode of procedure is indicative of the inability of the bishop to rule those subject to him without the intervention of the metropolitan or other bishops.

Savagnone's other argument to the effect that the provincial council possessed many of the powers which were later to be found belonging to the diocesan synod is perhaps more convincing. Thus, besides the alienation of Church property, contentious cases concerning religious observances [42] and disputes between clerics,[43] as well as criminal causes of the clergy,[44] were to be examined in the provincial council. This is entirely in accord with the evidence of ancient canon law on the important part the provincial council played in the life of the Church. It may very well be that because there was less need for its existence the diocesan synod did not originate in the empire but arose outside it at a later date. But it is another thing to say that it would be impossible because the metropolitan had complete authority over the bishops. The few references that are found in the sources are not a sufficient basis for so far-reaching a conclusion.

Article III. Early Legislation on the Diocesan Synod

In several of the councils held from the sixth century on, legislation was enacted in regard to the celebration of the synod. Thus it is possible to group these references together and obtain from them a general idea of how the synod gradually developed during this period. As a consequence more light will be thrown on the later general legislation.

The available evidence allows one to conclude that especially in France and Germany the synod was to be held regularly. In some places it was ordered to be celebrated immediately after the provincial council so that the legislation there enacted could be properly

[42] C. 23, C. Th., XVI, 2.

[43] Nov. 123, c. 10; Nov. 137, c. 4.

[44] Nov. 137, c. 4, 5. This later enactment was contrary to the text of the Theodosian Code, which removed all criminal cases from the competence of the synod.

promulgated.[45] At first this was twice a year, but afterwards in several places only once a year.[46] On the other hand, the synod was to be held in many other sections without any apparent connection with the provincial council, either once in the year [47] or twice a year.[48] Thus, while the idea of all the legislation was that there be a regular celebration of the synod, the prescribed frequency varied with the locality and the needs of the different sections.

In practically all of this legislation it is stated that the bishop was the one to convoke the synod. Upon him, therefore, was incumbent the duty of having the clergy present, since the very nature and purpose of the synod demanded their attendance.[49] They must become acquainted with recent provincial decrees, and besides they were to report to the bishop how they were carrying on their work in the ministry. At times, too, the abbots of the various monasteries in the diocese were to be summoned to assist in the deliberations.[50] Moreover there is evidence that even the laity were present in some instances.[51] Phillips [52] explains the presence of the laity by the fact that in several places the synod was the judiciary body, and accordingly the civil authorities would be present to execute the decisions.

[45] 16 Council of Toledo (693), c. 7—Mansi, XII, 74; 2 Council of Clovesho (747), c. 25—Mansi, XII, 403; 63 Epistle of Boniface—*M. P. L.*, LXXXIX, 764.

[46] Cf. Phillips, *Die Diöcesansynode*, p. 49.

[47] Synod of Auxerre (578), c. 7—Mansi, IX, 931; Council of Huesca (598), c. 1—Mansi, X, 481; Council of Germany (743), c. 1—Mansi, XII, 365; Council of Liptin (743), c. 1—Mansi, XII, 370; Council of Soissons (744), c. 2—Hefele-Leclerque, III, 856.

[48] Capitulary of Herardus, c. 91—*M. P. L.*, CXXI, 763; Capitulary of Otto, c. 27—*M. P. L.*, CXXXIV, 34 ff. Otto, Bishop of Vercelles, insists that even though it would be impossible to continue the former practice of holding the synod semi-annually, it should be convoked at least annually since it means so much for the welfare of the Church.

[49] Council of Metz (753), c. 3—Mansi, XII, 571; Council of Verdun (755), c. 8—Mansi, XII, 581.

[50] Council of Auxerre (578), subscription—Mansi, IX, 911-918; Council of Huesca (598), c. 1—Mansi, X, 481; 16 Council of Toledo (693), c. 7—Mansi, XII, 74.

[51] 16 Council of Toledo (693), c. 7—Mansi, XII, 74; Council of Salegunstadt (1022) appendix—Hardouin, VI a, 830.

[52] *Die Diöcesansynode*, p. 54.

Possibly, too, the people were summoned so that they would be informed of any new provincial ordinance that affected them directly. It must be admitted that it is difficult to determine the exact reason for their presence, and even to establish whether or not they had an active part in the synod. Thomassinus,[53] however, insists that the laity had no vote in any of the discussions.

The relation of the synod to the provincial council during this period has already been indicated. Under existing conditions a synodal assembly would be the easiest way to promulgate new provincial decrees and have knowledge of them carried to every part of the diocese. But, when in addition to this more particular legislation would be needed, there would be an additional reason for convoking the synod. The priests who came were to render to the bishop an account of how they were carrying on their work and then receive instructions as to what they should teach the laity and how they themselves should live.[54] In a few instances the synod was to formulate directions to be followed against heresies.[55] Probably, too, as Benedict XIV [56] suggests, several of the penitential books [57] were composed in the diocesan synod as statutes in regard to the Sacrament of Penance. They would be intended as a practical help for the clergy in determining who were worthy of absolution and what penance was to be demanded of them; and the synod would be an ideal place for the bishop to familiarize himself with the peculiar local conditions that had to be taken into account. In addition to this legislative work, apparently in some places the synod was also the dioc-

[53] *Vetus et Nova Disciplina de Beneficiis*, p. II, l. 3, c. 73, n. 3.

[54] Council of Huesca (598), c. 1—Mansi, X, 481; 4 Council of Toledo (633), c. 26—Mansi, X, 627; Council of Liptin (743), c. 3—Mansi, XII, 371; Council of Soissons (744), c. 4—Hefele-Leclerque, III, 856; Council of Clovesho (747), c. 25—Mansi, XII, 403; 6 Council of Arles (813), c. 4—Mansi, XIV, 59; Capitulary of Theodulphus, c. 28—*M. P. L.*, CV, 200; Capitulary of Otto, c. 27—*M. P. L.*, CXXXIV, 34 ff.

[55] Council of Soissons (744), c. 2—Hefele-Leclerque, III, 856; Council of Arras (1025), c. 1—Mansi, XIX, 43 ff.

[56] *De Synodo Dioecesana*, l. I, c. 1, n. 7.

[57] Cf. Brat, *Les Livres Pénitentiaux et La Pénitence Tarifée*, p. 11; Van Hove, *Prolegomena ad Codicem*, p. 119; Cicognani, *Jus Canonicum*, I, 245.

esan judiciary.[58] The passage of the *Breviarium Alarici* already referred to would indicate this. Probably, however, only the cases that directly concerned the clergy were taken up there, since generally speaking they were the only members.

A word remains to be said about the form that the synodal legislation took. Even as early as the eighth century this was drafted into diocesan statutes which were called *capitula synodalia*.[59] Several of these have come down to the present day, among which are the capitularies of Theodulphus of Orleans,[60] Herardus of Tours,[61] Hincmar of Rheims,[62] Riculfus of Soissons,[63] and Otto of Vercelles.[64] According to Thomassinus[65] both Herardus and Hincmar promulgated their capitularies by having them read to all present at the synod; and this may have been the mode of promulgation used by the others.

[58] Thomassinus, *Vetus et Nova Disciplina*, p. II, 1. 3, c. 73, n. 5; c. 75, n. 3; *Le Canoniste Contemporain*, XLVI (1924), 255.

[59] Cf. Mansi, XVIII b, 77, 627; Capitulary of Herardus, praefatio—*M. P. L.*, CXXI, 765; Van Hove, *Prolegomena ad Codicem*, p. 118.

[60] *M. P. L.*, CV, 191 ff.

[61] *M. P. L.*, CXXI, 763 ff.

[62] Mansi, XV, 475, 493, 503.

[63] *M. P. L.*, CXXXI, 191 ff.

[64] *M. P. L.*, CXXXIV, 27 ff.

[65] *Vetus et Nova Disciplina*, p. II, 1. 3, c. 74, n. 7.

CHAPTER III

GENERAL LEGISLATION ON THE DIOCESAN SYNOD

THE celebration of the diocesan synod was not enjoined by general law until the thirteenth century. But even previous to that, records indicate that in very many sections the synod was held regularly.[1] It seems that national and provincial councils had come to appreciate the usefulness of the synod for the welfare of the Church and had imposed its celebration. Very probably, too, in many places this practice was adopted by various bishops, who recognized the value of the synod. Continuing thus for a considerable period of time the frequent celebration of the synod might be accepted as a custom having the force of a law. This may be the reason Gratian included in his *Decretum* previous legislation on the synod.[2] He probably found it as a sufficiently widespread practice to be able to regard it as very similar to a general law.

ARTICLE I. ANTE-TRIDENTINE LEGISLATION

The first general law on the diocesan synod might be interpreted as directed to suppress heresy. For the Fourth Lateran Council (1215), held principally in opposition to the heresy of the Albigenses, imposed the celebration of the synod on the entire Church.[3] This enactment was identical with the legislation already in force in many places. The synod was to be held each year immediately after the provincial council had been celebrated, in order to promulgate the legislation there enacted for the province. Previous to the provincial

[1] Cf. Migne, *Encyclopedie Théologique,* XIV, 1350-57; Mansi, XXXVI, 73-120, 323-330.

[2] C. 16, D. XVIII. According to the text this was taken from a *Concilium Bylonense.* There is, however, no record of any such council, and so authors have suggested two hypotheses: that it was taken either from canon 5 of the *Breviarium Hipponense* (393) or from the introduction of the *Concilium Cabilonense* (649). Cf. Savagnone, *Studi in Onore di Biagio Brugi,* pp. 582-83.

[3] C. 6—Mansi, XXII, 991.

council a certain number of the clergy were to be appointed who would investigate conditions in their respective dioceses and then report their findings to the council. There steps were to be taken to eradicate the abuses that had been reported. But in order to insure the effectiveness of these ordinances, it was deemed necessary to have them promulgated in annual episcopal synods, because this would be the only way to have the knowledge of the decrees reach all parts of each diocese. The Lateran law concluded with the declaration of a penalty. Whoever violated any of the prescriptions was to be suspended, as long as his superior thought it prudent, from both his office and benefices.[4]

Although this law ordained that the synod was to be held once a year, it cannot be concluded that it forbade a semi-annual celebration wherever this had been the practice. Rather it seems, as Phillips [5] points out, that those places in which this had been the practice were free to continue it. Thus several councils renewed "the ancient practice" of celebrating the synod semi-annually unless circumstances allowed only an annual celebration.[6] Such legislation could not be considered contrary to the law but rather *beside* the law; for apparently the fathers of the Lateran Council did not intend that the practice of the semi-annual celebration of synods be abrogated. They rather wished to prescribe the minimum which had to be observed than interfere where what they were striving to stabilize was very faithfully practiced.

The next few centuries brought no change in this legislation. In fact all that is recorded is a reiteration of the Lateran law together with regulations about the membership of the synod. Accordingly one finds that the law on the provincial council and the diocesan synod was incorporated as a separate chapter in the Decretals of

[4] The text of the penalty "suspendatur" implies that it was only *ferendae sententiae*. Cf. Fagnanus, *Commentarium in Libros Decretalium*, 1. 5, c. XXV, 105 ff.

[5] *Die Diöcesansynode*, p. 64. Cf. Cappello, *De Visitatione Liminum*, I, 304.

[6] Council of Clermont (1268) preface—Mansi, XXIII, 1185; Council of Copenhagen (1425)—Mansi, XXVIII, 1092; 1 Council of Cologne (1536), XIV, 17-18—Mansi, XXXII, 1292; 2 Council of Cologne (1549) V, 1—Mansi, XXXII, 1385; Synod of Tolouse (1531)—cf. Pistocchi, *De Synodo Dioecesana*, p. 11.

Gregory IX [7] and imposed anew as general law. Besides, in the Decretals as well as in the Liber Sextus of Boniface VIII, regulations were laid down in regard to the attendance of abbots at the synod.[8] The other details, however, were still left to be determined by local legislation or practice.

The Council of Basle (1433-1437), which was convoked principally to initiate some needed reforms, was the next to treat of the synod.[9] It was stated that an episcopal synod was to be celebrated each year, preferably after the octave of Easter, unless there existed the custom of celebrating it semi-annually. The bishop was personally to supervise the celebration of the synod; and only when it was impossible for him to do this was he allowed to delegate another.[10] In case a bishop neglected this duty, the provincial council was to investigate the matter and punish the delinquent. At first he was to be deprived of the revenues of all his benefices; and, if after three months he was still contumacious, suspension both from his office and his benefices was to be imposed. Then it devolved upon the senior bishop to have the synod celebrated. The object of the synod was to correct abuses in the diocese. In it a detailed account was to be made concerning the administration of the sacraments, the moral condition of the laity, the existence of heresy and superstitious practices, and the observance by religious of their rules. In order to insure an exact report for succeeding synods, officials known as *synodal witnesses* were to be appointed whose sole duty for the ensuing year was to investigate these conditions in the diocese. It was

[7] C. 25, X, *de accusationibus, inquisitionibus et denunciationibus*, V, 1. The suspension previously threatened was here changed to suspension from office only. But it still remained *ferendae sententiae*—"suspendatur ab officio."

[8] C. 9, X, *de majoritate et obedientia*, I, 33; c. 7, X, *de privilegiis et excessibus privilegiatorum*, V, 33; c. 6, *de privilegiis*, V, 7 in VI°.

[9] Session 15—Mansi, XXIV, 74 ff. Since this council ended up as schismatical, it is generally agreed that its decrees never became general law. Cf. Van Hove, *Prolegomena*, p. 192. However, Cicognani (*Jus Canonicum*, I, 181) on the authority of Hefele seems to imply that the decrees of the first twenty-five sessions received papal approbation.

[10] In one place, although no enumeration is given, mention is made of those being present who were bound to attend. Probably the exact membership was still to be determined by local regulation and custom.

also stated that the other diocesan officials were to assist in this investigation.

These prescriptions were certainly a very effective program of the reform which everyone saw was imperative. Even if they never became general law, it is unfortunate that bishops did not follow their provisions. Likewise it is regrettable that the similar attempt of Leo X in the Fifth Lateran Council [11] to use the diocesan synod as an instrument of reform was also abortive. Without a doubt the observance of this practice would have forestalled a good part of the later disasters.

Article II. Tridentine Legislation

The reforms in ecclesiastical discipline which were adopted in the Council of Trent were intended to eradicate the evils which the so-called reformers had used as a pretext for their revolt. For many reasons, but particularly because of the inevitable pagan influence of the Renaissance, there had been an almost unbelievable apathy to conditions. Undoubtedly there were many who did their utmost to reform at least within the sphere of their own influence. But more than that was needed in order to insure that similar conditions would not arise within another century when the feeling of indignation had subsided. It was necessary to initiate a thorough reform in the discipline of the Church by renewing and strengthening the force of the former laws, and by guaranteeing a lasting observance of new regulations to be adopted.

Many realized that one of the means to bring about this effective reformation was to insist again on the celebration of the diocesan synod. The synod had never been held regularly, but at the time even less attention was paid it.[12] Insistence upon it once more was apt to reawaken all to its importance. This undoubtedly was the reason Fredericus Nausea, bishop of Vienne, declared in his report to Paul III that the failure of so many bishops in not only not attending the synod but even in not having it celebrated was one of the abuses that had to be reformed; and therefore he requested

[11] "*Regimini universali,*" 10th Sess.—Mansi, XXXII, 907.

[12] Cf. Migne, *Encyclopedie Théologique,* XIV, 1387 ff.; Mansi, XXXVI a, 203 ff., 336 ff.

legislation on this matter.[13] A similar petition was contained in the recommendations made by the French king to the council when legislation on the synod and the provincial council was requested.[14] In Germany steps had already been taken in this direction when the *Formula Reformationis* [15] of Charles V, which was promulgated in 1548 at the Diet of Augsburg, prescribed the regular celebration of the synod as a means of reform. It was, therefore, to be expected that same similar enactment would be made at Trent.

In the draft of the second of the twenty-one canons of reformation, submitted in the twenty-fourth session to the commission of bishops for examination and criticism, it was stated that episcopal synods were to be held annually, to which all the clergy were bound to come except those subject to a general chapter and without a parochial office.[16] The penalty of suspension from office which had been decreed formerly was renewed against those who violated this ordinance. When asked for their comments on these proposals, several bishops suggested changes. Some thought it advisable to hold the synod less frequently,[17] while one bishop wanted a semi-annual celebration.[18] Then, too, suggestions were made that legislation be enacted about some details of the celebration.[19] But the final decision was to adopt what had been originally proposed, and accordingly it became general law as part of the twenty canons of reformation promulgated in the twenty-fourth session. The only change made from the original draft was in the wording to make its sense clear.

In several other parts of its decrees the Council gave instructions about some matters to be settled in the synod. In the first synod of each diocese after the Council had ended, all who were bound to be

13 *Conc. Tridentini Diariorum, Actorum, Epistolarum, Tractatuum Nova Collectio*, XII, 400, 419.

14 *Postul. Oratorum Reg. Gall.*, Act. Petit. 34, as quoted by Phillips, *Die Diöcesansynode*, p. 83, n. 4. Cf. Benedict XIV, *De Synodo Dioecesana*, 1. 1, c. 6, n. 4.

15 Title 21—Phillips, *Die Diöcesansynode*, p. 74.

16 *Conc. Tridentini Diariorum . . . Nova Collectio*, IX, 750.

17 *Conc. Tridentini Diariorum . . . Nova Collectio*, IX, 825-26, 864.

18 *Conc. Tridentini Diariorum . . . Nova Collectio*, IX, 859.

19 *Conc. Tridentini Diariorum . . . Nova Collectio*, IX, 850, 857.

present were to accept publicly what had been decreed there, to profess allegiance to the Pope, and to renounce all the heresies but particularly those condemned during the Council.[20] In chapter four of the same session bishops were given power to ordain in the synod as they saw fit with regard to bequests for masses for churches whenever either all the masses could not be taken care of on the days set by the donors or the stipends were so small that it was difficult to get priests to assume responsibility for these masses. The other regulations concerned the appointment of synodal judges and the examiners in the concursus for vacant parishes. The former were to be named in the synod after those present had expressed their choice in the form of a consultative vote.[21] In the appointment of the latter the members of the synod also had only a consultative vote except in the case of examiners in the concursus for vacant parishes when they had a decisive vote.[22]

Article III. Post-Tridentine Regulations

The period that followed the Council of Trent brought no change in the legislation on the diocesan synod. What was there enacted, which of course was practically the same legislation as had been binding since the thirteenth century, was not revoked until the promulgation of the Code. There were, however, two matters not treated at the Council about which definite provisions were made during this period. The first concerned the liturgical celebration of the synod. Details about this were given in the *Pontificale Romanum* [23] and in the *Ceremoniale Episcoporum*,[24] both of which were issued by Clement VIII and revised under several of the succeeding pontiffs. But since this matter is not canonical, it is outside the scope of this study. The other regulation, which determined who was the legislator in the synod, should be examined more closely.

[20] Sessio XXV, *de reformatione*, c. 2.

[21] Sessio XXV, *de reformatione*, c. 10. Cf. Benedict XIV, *De Synodo Dioecesana*, l. iv, c. 5, n. 5.

[22] Sessio XXIII, *de reformatione*, c. 7, 15; sess. XXIV, *de reformatione*, c. 18. Cf. Benedict XIV, *De Synodo Dioecesana*, l. iv, c. 7, n. 2.

[23] Pars 3.

[24] l. I, c. 3.

From the sixteenth century on there had been some who considered the synod to be a legislative body in which all present have a decisive vote.[25] Such a considerable number of the clergy insisted on this as their right that many bishops, in order to forestall possible trouble, deemed it more advisable to convoke the synod as infrequently as possible. This is one of the reasons why the Tridentine law was so little observed. When bishops did convoke synods, disputes about this point arose, and on several occasions the Holy See was called upon to give a decision. The substance of the replies was that, despite the fact that the Roman Pontifical stated that the synodal constitutions were to be confirmed by the clergy, it was not necessary for the validity of this legislation to obtain their consent, and moreover that, although the bishops should consult the chapter about these enactments, it was not necessary, despite any contrary custom, to follow their advice except in the cases stated by law.[26] Of themselves these particular decisions had the force of law only for those to whom they were given. However the exclusive legislative power of the bishop was enunciated in all. Consequently this principle had legal value as a customary ordinance of the Congregation (*stylus Curiae*). Accordingly Pius VI condemned the contrary propositions of the Synod of Pistoia (1786).[27] Because the principle was being frequently denied, he believed it necessary to declare it beyond all doubt.

Besides this general provision there were several particular declarations of the Holy See in regard to other questions related to the diocesan synod. For the most part these did not state the general

[25] Cf. Wernz-Vidal, *De Personis*, p. 622; De Meester, *Juris Canonici Compendium*, II, 713; *Le Canoniste Contemporain*, XLVI (1924), 257; Oesterle, *Praelectiones Juris Canonici*, I, 181-182.

[26] S. C. C. *Urgellen.*, 1581—*Fontes*, n. 2134; S. C. C. *Venetiarum*, 21 April, 1592—*Fontes*, n. 2243; S. C. C. *Algaren.*, 12 Jan., 1595—*Fontes*, n. 2278; S. C. C. *Nullius*, 1 July, 1597—*Fontes*, n. 2315; S. C. C. *Januen.*, 2 Dec., 1604 ad 1—*Fontes*, n. 2353; S. C. C. *Oriolen.*, 26 July, 1614—*Fontes*, n. 2395; S. C. C. *Burgen.*, 5 June, 1627—*Fontes*, n. 2481; S. C. C. *Savonen.*, 19 Feb., 1628—*Fontes*, n. 2488; S. C. C. *Oriolen.*, 27 May, 1632 ad 15—*Fontes*, n. 2543; S. C. C. *Cortonen.*, 27 May, 1702—*Fontes*, n. 2994; S. C. C. *Gerunden.*, 19 Dec., 1739 ad 4;—Richter, *Canones et Decreta Conc. Tridentini*, p. 330.

[27] Const. "*Auctorem fidei*," 28 Aug. 1794, prop. Synodi Pistorien. damn., prop. 9, 10—*Fontes*, n. 475.

law, for they were only responses to the questions of individuals. Nevertheless they are valuable. They indicate how the Church viewed these matters, and therefore help one to understand the legislation that has since come into force.

A few of the declarations were clearly nothing more than a reiteration of what had already been decreed at the Council of Trent, and consequently must be accepted as what obliged the entire Church. Such were the declarations of several popes who insisted on the regular celebration of the synod [28] as well as the decisions that reaffirmed that regulars who had the care of souls were obliged to attend the synod.[29] The remaining responses were extensive in character. That is, they laid down regulations to which no reference had been made in the Tridentine law. These, therefore, had the force of law only for those to whom they were addressed.[30] First of all in regard to the right of convocation, it was decided that an abbot, even with quasi-episcopal jurisdiction or the right to conduct the concursus for vacant benefices, had not the power to convoke the synod unless he was given this privilege by the Holy See,[31] and that a vicar general had this right only when he had a special mandate from the bishop.[32] The bishop alone had this power, and it was even decided that he could exercise it without the consent of his chapter unless it could prove that the necessity of its consent was a legitimate custom still reasonable.[33] In addition to this group of decisions, there were others given concerning the attendance of the synod

[28] Pius IX, ep. encycl. *"Singulari quidem,"* 17 March 1856—*Fontes,* n. 521; *"Cum nuper,"* 20 Jan. 1858—*Fontes,* n. 523; Leo XIII, const. *"Romanos Pontifices,"* 8 May 1881—*Fontes,* n. 582.

[29] S. C. C., 19 Dec. 1604—*Fontes,* n. 2354; S. C. C. *Passov.,* 1 Oct. 1667—Richter, *Canones et Decreta Conc. Tridentini,* p. 330.

[30] Cf. Choupin, *Valeur de Decisions Doctrinales et Disciplinaires,* pp. 96-105.

[31] S. C. C. *Nullius,* 17 Aug. 1626—Richter, *Canones et Decreta Conc. Tridentini,* p. 328; S. C. C. *Nullius a. Messan,* 5 July 1738—*Thesaurus Resolutionum S. C. Concilii ad annum 1738,* p. 106.

[32] S. C. C. *Nullius,* 4 Dec. 1655—*Fontes,* n. 2745.

[33] S. C. C. *Verodunen.,* Dec. 1585—*Fontes,* n. 2149; S. C. C. *Calaritana,* 16 July 1599—*Fontes,* n. 2327; S. C. C. *Oriolen.,* 27 May 1632 ad 14—*Fontes,* n. 2543; S. C. C. *Fulginaten.,* 26 Feb. 1639—*Fontes,* n. 2602.

and the bishop's power, if need be, to oblige the clergy to come.[34] A bishop was allowed to compel by ecclesiastical censures the cathedral chapter [35] and regulars who were in charge of parishes [36] to attend the synod. Whether or not a bishop could force the superior of regulars in charge of parishes to be present seemed to depend on the circumstances of each case, since the decisions differed.[37] Ordinarily a bishop was not to oblige under penalty the clergy with simple benefices or those without any benefice to attend the synod. However he could do this when a matter of general reformation or one that affected the entire body of clergy was to be discussed, or when the decrees of the provincial council were to be promulgated.[38] The remaining matter submitted for settlement was the case in which two dioceses were united and it was not known whether or not it was necessary to hold a synod in each diocese. The tenor of the decisions appears to have been that if the dioceses were united *aeque principaliter* one synod was sufficient; although, because of special circumstances, in several cases two distinct synods were ordered. On the other hand, if one diocese was of greater dignity, one synod could be held there for each diocese.[39]

Before concluding this article it is necessary to say a word about

[34] S. C. C. *Forosempron.*, 17 Jan. 1654—Richter, *Canones et Decreta Conc. Tridentini*, p. 329.

[35] S. C. C. *Oriolen.*, 27 May 1632 ad 19—*Fontes*, n. 2543.

[36] S. C. C., 19 Dec. 1604—*Fontes*, n. 2354; S. C. C. *Passov.*, 1 Oct. 1667—Richter, *Canones et Decreta Conc. Tridentini*, p. 330; Clement XIII, const. "*Inter multiplices*," 11 Dec. 1758—*Fontes*, n. 449.

[37] S. C. C. *Cremon.*, 15 May 1574—*Fontes*, n. 2128; S. C. C. *Segovien.*, 1 April 1656—*Fontes*, n. 2747; S. C. C. *Cremon.*, 5 April 1732—*Fontes*, n. 3387; S. C. C. *Cremon.*, 8 et 29 Aug. 1733—*Fontes*, n. 3407.

[38] S. C. C. *Ferrarien.*, 24 Sept. 1591—Cappello, *De Visitatione Liminum*, I, 308; S. C. C. *Tulen.*, 17 March 1593—Richter, *Canones et Decreta Conc. Tridentini*, p. 329; S. C. C. *Januen.*, 10 Sept. 1633—*Fontes*, n. 2555; S. C. C. *Forosempronien.*, 17 Jan. 1654—Cappello *(l. c.)*.

[39] S. C. C. *Pennen. et Adrien.*, 16 April 1622—Richter, *Canones et Decreta Conc. Tridentini*, p. 36; S. C. C. *Geruntinen et Cariaten.*, 11 Feb. 1708—*Fontes*, n. 3061; S. C. C. *Terracinen.*, *Setina, et Prevernen.*, 1 Mar. 1766 ad 5 et 6—*Thesaurus Resolutionum S. C. Concilii ad annum 1766*, p. 53 ff. Cf. also Pallotini, *Collectio Omnium Conclusionum et Resolutionum S. C. Concilii*, XVI, 596, note 3.

the tentative legislation on the diocesan synod which was prepared in the Vatican Council. The first draft of the section entitled: *Schema constitutionis de episcopis, de synodis et de vicariis generalibus* contained a chapter on the synod.[40] It was proposed that, in order to make the celebration of the synod easier, it need be held only every three years and when, because of special circumstances, even this was impossible the Holy See was to be consulted as to the provisions that must be made. The framers of this proposal took into account the fact that the Tridentine law was not being observed; and they therefore suggested a mitigation to meet the changed conditions.[41] The bishops who examined this draft were for the most part satisfied with the provision of the synod. Some requests were made, however, that the synod be held even less frequently and that only a part of the clergy be obliged to come.[42] The adoption of either of these suggestions would provide a way out of many of the difficulties that had attended the previously required celebration. But, except for the assertion that the bishop was the only legislator in the synod, the second draft prepared was substantially the same as the first.[43] Owing to the premature closing of the council the prescriptions never became law. However they show another development in the evolution of the present discipline.

Article IV. Juridical Aspect of the Non-Observance of the Tridentine Law

The topic of this final article is whether or not the fact that diocesan synods were not generally held as the Tridentine law prescribed had any effect on the law itself. Formerly there were several canonists who maintained that the continuous practice of non-observance gave rise to a contrary custom [44] and they therefore believed that it was no longer obligatory to hold the synod each year. By far the majority of canonists, however, did not consider that

[40] Mansi, L, 345 ff.

[41] Mansi, L, 351 ff.

[42] Mansi, L, 868 ff.

[43] Mansi, LIII, 721.

[44] Cf. Benedict XIV, *De Synodo Dioecesana,* l. 1, c. 6, n. 6; Cappello, *De Visitatione Liminum,* I, 321.

such a deduction was justified, although all conceded some mitigation.[45] Just how much one may admit will be best determined by a consideration of all the facts.

There is little need to go into detail to prove that the Tridentine law on the diocesan synod was not observed. However, a distinction must be made. Immediately after the Council of Trent, synods were held as the law prescribed throughout practically the entire Church.[46] But such faithful observance did not continue for long. Even as early as the middle of the eighteenth century Benedict XIV [47] deplored the fact that this law was not observed; and a little later in the same century Van Espen [48] wrote that it was disregarded practically everywhere and that in some dioceses a synod had not been held in more than fifty years.[49] The same condition continued until about the middle of the nineteenth century, when many bishops attempted to convoke synods as often as circumstances permitted.[50] Even then the Holy See and many plenary and provincial councils found it necessary to urge the more frequent celebration of the synod, and authors who wrote on the synod did not fail to discuss the marked non-observance of the Tridentine law.

Such a condition continued for several centuries. Would it not, therefore, be correct to conclude that a contrary practice had nullified the law to some extent? At first sight it would appear that an affirmative answer must be given. But after a little consideration one realizes that there are other facts to which attention must be

45 Cf. e. g. Benedict XIV (*l. c.*); Santi, *Praelectiones Juris Canonici,* 1. 1, t. 31, n. 176; Wernz, *Jus Decretalium,* IIb, 861; Claeys-Bouuaert, *De Canonica Cleri Saecularis Obedientia,* p. 86; Bouix, *De Episcopo,* II, 351 ff.; Cappello, *De Visitatione Liminum,* I, 320-323.

46 Cf. Mansi, XXXVI a, 234 ff.; Calenzio, *Documenti Inediti sul Concilio di Trento,* p. 575 ff.

47 *De Synodo Dioecesana,* 1. I, c. 6, n. 5.

48 *Jus Ecclesiasticum Universum,* p. I, t. 18, n. 6.

49 Oesterle (*Praelectiones Juris Canonici,* I, 181) gives the following reasons for this almost complete non-observance: concentration of episcopal powers, institution of the diocesan curia, possibility of printing new decrees, the fact that many bishops were temporal rulers and thus took little interest in their ecclesiastical duties, cumulation of many dioceses by one bishop, and interference of the secular power.

50 Cf. Mansi, XXXVI a, 270-338.

paid. No conclusion is justifiable unless these are taken into account.

The first fact is that the Holy See did not consider that the Tridentine law on the diocesan synod had been changed by custom. It is true that it never explicitly stated that this was not so. But it is clearly implied in many of its declarations. The Popes on several occasions exhorted the bishops of different sections of the Church to be diligent in celebrating the synod, which should be held *according to the command of the canons.*[51] A similar implication apparently is contained in the exhortation of the Sacred Congregation of the Council to several bishops, after their report of the condition of their dioceses, to hold the synod when they judged it expedient for the spiritual good of their diocese, even though it did not insist on the observance of the Tridentine law in the presence of extraordinary circumstances.[52] The same attitude is implied in the decree of December 31, 1909, "A remotissima," of the Sacred Consistorial Congregation [53] which was to be answered by the bishops in reporting the conditions of the diocese. Finally, the fact that many bishops were granted indults which allowed them to restrict the number of the clergy who would be obliged to go to the synod so that its annual celebration would be less difficult, seems to indicate that the Holy See must not have considered that the law on the diocesan synod had been changed.[54] Evidently its attitude was the same as

[51] Sixtus V, const. "*Immensa*"—cf. Cappello, *De Visitatione Liminum,* I, 322; Benedict XIV, ep. encycl. "*Quamvis paternae,*" 26 Aug. 1741—*Fontes,* n. 315; Pius IX, "*Nostris quidem,*" 8 Dec. 1849—cf. Cappello, *l. c.;* Pius IX, ep. encycl. "*Cum nuper,*" 20 Jan. 1858—*Fontes,* n. 523; Leo XIII, const. "*Romanos Pontifices,*" 8 May 1881—*Fontes,* n. 582.

[52] Cf. Santi, *Praelectiones Juris Canonici,* 1. I, t. 31, n. 176.

[53] *A. A. S.,* II, 20.

[54] Indult to Bishop of Liège, 4 May 1851—Claeys-Bouuaert, *De Canonica Cleri Saecularis Obedientia,* p. 87; Letter of Pius IX to hierarchy of Austria, 5 Nov. 1855—*Collectio Lacensis,* V, 1239, 1251; Indult to the Bishop of Iglesias, 1860, and to Archbishop of Mechlin, 1872—cf. *Le Canoniste Contemporain,* XII (1889), 148; Indult to Bishop of Namur—cf. Claeys-Bouuaert *(l. c.);* Indult to Bishop of Bayonne, 16 Feb. 1889—*A. S. S.,* XXI, 726-729; Indult to Bishop of Brescia, 6 July 1889—*A. S. S.,* XXII, 350-355; Letter of S. C. de Prop. Fide to Archbishop of Milwaukee, 29 July 1889—*Collectanea,*

that of the fathers of the Vatican Council; namely, that the Tridentine law was to be observed whenever prevailing obstacles could be overcome.

There is another fact of almost equal importance which has to be considered. In many plenary and provincial councils held during the nineteenth century in practically every part of the Church the bishops were directed by the decrees of the councils to hold the diocesan synod annually. And what is more important, reference was often explicity made to the Tridentine law as obliging to the celebration of the synod.[55] Of course cognizance was taken of the difficulties that often had to be met with in the celebration of the synod. Yet every bishop was urged to strive as earnestly as possible to obey the law which Trent had laid down. If such strong insistence was made despite the many evident obstacles, it is clear that it was done because the law of Trent was considered as still binding in its entirety whenever it was possible to abide by its precepts. It does not appear to imply that a change in the law followed its nonobservance.

In the light of these facts, therefore, it does not seem that the Tridentine law about the diocesan synod was ever changed by a

2276; Indult to Plenary Council of Latin America, 1 Jan. 1900—*Le Canoniste Contemporain,* XXIII (1900), 368-371; Indult to Bishop of Marianna, 29 July 1905—*Thesaurus Resolutionum S. C. Concilii ad annum 1905,* 846 ff.; Faculties to Bishops of Latin America and Philippine Islands, 1 Jan. 1910—*Le Canoniste Contemporain,* XXXIII (1910), 313-315.

[55] Council of Posonia (1822)—*Collectio Lacensis,* V, 939; Gathering of Bishops at Würzburg, sess. XXIV (*l. c.*), 979; Plenary Council of Thurles (1850) XX, 5, (*l. c.*), III, 791; Council of Quebec (1851) XIX—(*l. c.*), 616; 1 Council of Westminister XXIX, 5—(*l. c.*), 946; Council of Cashel (1853) 5—(*l. c.*), 842; Council of Tuam (1854) XXIII—(*l. c.*), 863; Council of Ravenna (1855), XIII—(*l. c.*), IV, 189; 1 Council of Halifax (1857) XIX, 6—(*l. c.*), III, 755; Council of Strigonia (1858) IX, 5—(*l. c.*), V, 87 ff.; Council of Urbina (1859) CVI, p. 4, c. 2—(*l. c.*), VI, 37; Council of Vienne (1859) II, 11—(*l. c.*), VI, 159; Council of Utrecht (1865) II, 4—(*l. c.*), 783; II Plenary Council of Baltimore (1866) n. 63—*Concilii Plenarii Baltimorensis II Acta et Decreta,* p. 50; Plenary Council of Latin America (1899) n. 284-288—*Acta et Decreta Concilii Plenarii Americae Latinae,* pp. 132 ff.; III Plenary Council of Australia (1905), n. 33, 82, 240—*Acta et Decreta Concilii Plenarii Australiensis III,* pp. 15, 34, 80.

general custom.[56] The reason in support of this deduction is the fact that the consent of the legislator, which must be at the basis of every legally established custom, was not given to this practice. While, of course, no express reprobation of the custom was made in any declaration of the Holy See, nevertheless because the existence of the law was reiterated on several occasions it seems correct to maintain that the evident implication was that a contrary practice had no legal value. On the contrary, if there was a legally established custom in force, it would seem that this exception would be referred to in one of the declarations. Since it was not, one may conclude that there was not such a custom. Besides, because the hierarchy of practically the entire Church acknowledged the binding force of the Tridentine law in their respective conciliary gatherings, it is clear that there was no intention on their part to introduce a contrary custom. Yet this is essential in establishing a legal custom. When, therefore, instead of acceptance of the practice one finds determined reprobation of the non-observance, except when necessitated by unusual conditions, the only conclusion appears to be that a contrary custom could not have been introduced. The fact of non-observance by itself was insufficient to change the law.

A conclusion about the entire question can be drawn only when a distinction has been made. Since the Tridentine law prescribing the annual celebration of the synod apparently was not changed by custom, one must conclude that those bishops who, had they wished, were able to convoke the synod annually and yet failed to do so cannot be excused. They were not fulfilling one of the important obligations of the episcopal office; for they violated without proportionate reason a law which the Church had insisted on for several centuries. It was to them that Benedict XIV [57] spoke when he reproved and held as inexecusable those bishops who through care-

[56] Because the Rota and the Congregation of the Council usually refused to admit customs contrary to the Tridentine discipline, some authors have denied that a contrary custom could ever have legal force. Nevertheless, since the value of immemorial contrary customs was recognized in a few decisions of the Rota, some mitigation was possible through custom. Cf. Michiels, *Normae Generales*, I, 105-106.

[57] *De Synodo Dioecesana*, l. I, c. 6, n. 5.

lessness failed to celebrate the synod and reminded them that besides their disobedience they were liable to suspension from office.

On the other hand, the case of bishops who found it difficult to hold the synod must be judged differently. There can be no doubt that the great majority of bishops wished to observe this law, but they could not for various reasons. They had to contend with such circumstances as troublous political conditions, governmental interference, scarcity of priests, vastness of their diocese and the error that priests had legislative power in the synod. If synods were held under such conditions more harm than good would result, and therefore it was advisable to delay their celebration. The Holy See realized these facts, and all that was done was to urge the bishops to make the best of circumstances and to hold the synod whenever it would be prudent. At times indults were given so that the synod could be held more easily. The bishops who did not receive such concessions were *per se* obliged to celebrate the synod according to the prescriptions of law. But, if conditions in their diocese were such that this could be done only with great difficulty, according to the accepted canonical principle of epikeia they were freed from such an obligation as long as these difficulties continued. It would be contrary to canonical equity and the reasonably interpreted wish of the legislator to prescribe the synod in such cases. When, however, these conditions ceased and the law could be more easily followed, the synod was to be held annually according to law. In the meantime, apparently the mind of the Holy See was that a bishop should hold the synod whenever he prudently could. As a substitute during the intervals between synods authors [58] proposed either the occasion of the clerical retreat or clerical conferences, or the calling together of the deans or senior clergy. For the mind of the Holy See [59] appeared to be that such dioceses should not be completely deprived of the benefits of the synod.

[58] Benedict XIV, *De Synodo Dioecesana*, 1. I, c. 2, n. 5; Claeys-Bouuaert, *De Canonica Cleri Saecularis Obedientia*, p. 89; Cappello, *De Visitatione Liminum*, I, 323.

[59] S. C. C. Caroniensis, 1720—Benedict XIV (*l. c.*); S. Cons. Cong. decree "*A remotissima*"—*A. A. S.*, II (1920), 20.

RÉSUMÉ

Such was the evolution which legislation on the diocesan synod had undergone up to the time of the promulgation of the Code. Apparently arising sometime after the fourth century, the synod had spread through the Church in the West, particularly in France and Germany, as an effective means of promulgating new provincial decrees as well as of keeping a vigilant watch over diocesan conditions and of even formulating the more specific and particular regulations that were needed. Then, because its advantages came to be better realized, in the thirteenth century the annual celebration of the synod was imposed by a general law which was reiterated by succeeding pontiffs at times when the synod could have been well used to bring about many urgently needed reforms. With a similar purpose uppermost in their minds the fathers of the Council of Trent renewed the past discipline, and in addition prescribed the attendance of all the clergy actively engaged in the ministry. In the mind of the Church the synod had become an integral part of her life, and she was anxious that her hierarchy be diligent in celebrating it regularly.

Side by side with the repeated insistency on the part of the legislator there was a general failure in practically every part of the Church to observe the law consistently. It may be said safely that at no time was there a general faithful observance. It would seem, however, that usually such a condition was not blameworthy. Among other things it can be explained for the most part by the difficulties that existed in meeting the reguirements demanded by the legislation on the synod. It was therefore to be expected that, as the fathers of the Vatican Council proposed, there should be some mitigation of the discipline on the synod in the Code of Canon Law, in order that its celebration would be made easier for dioceses of large size and those in which there was a scarcity of priests. A change of this kind would accomodate the legislation to modified conditions, and induce bishops not to deprive their dioceses of the benefits of the synod.

PART II

LEGISLATION OF THE CODE

CHAPTER IV

THE CONVOCATION OF THE SYNOD

Canon 356. § 1. In singulis dioecesibus celebranda est decimo saltem quoque anno dioecesana Synodus, in qua de iis tantum agendum quae ad particulares cleri populique dioecesis necessitates vel utilitates referuntur.

§ 2. Si Episcopus plures dioeceses aeque principaliter unitas regat, aut unam habeat in titulum, alteram aliasve in perpetuam administrationem, potest unam tantum dioecesanam Synodum ex omnibus dioecesibus convocare.

Canon 357. § 1. Synodum dioecesanam convocat eique praeest Episcopus, non autem Vicarius Generalis sine mandato speciali nec Vicarius Capitularis.

§ 2. Celebranda est in ecclesia cathedrali, nisi aliud rationabilis causa suadeat.

This chapter on the convocation of the synod will consist of four articles: (1) the obligation of convoking the synod; (2) the author of the synod; (3) its frequency; (4) the place of the synod.

Article I. Obligation of the Synod

1. *In Each Diocese*

The opening words of canon 356 § 1 state clearly the present grave obligation to celebrate the diocesan synod. This law renews an obligation binding the entire Church since the beginning of the thirteenth century. In the Code, however, changes have been made with regard to some details; namely, the frequency of the synod and the members who must be present. These mitigations had been foreshadowed by previous indults of the Holy See to several bishops and by legislation on the synod proposed in the Vatican Council.

In order to revive the synod, however, and establish it as an integral part of Church government, the requirements of the Code are even less stringent.

The words *"in singulis dioecesibus"* emphasize the attention which the legislator wishes to be paid to the celebration of the synod. It is obligatory in every diocese. It must be noted, however, that the text of the ordinance is expressed impersonally, and therefore a bishop is only indirectly bound by it. He need not personally supervise the celebration of the synod, although that is preferable. What is important is that the diocese have the synod. Neither the smallness nor the vastness of the territory can be a sufficient excuse. Once a diocese has been duly erected by the Holy See, the holding of the synod becomes obligatory. Moreover, any appeal to what might be considered a legally established particular custom as relieving from this obligation is manifestly of no value. The Code has made many notable changes in its legislation on the synod. It has removed practically all the difficulties which might prudently warrant the toleration of a contrary custom.[1] It must be said, then, that *per se* every diocese is obliged to hold the synod in order to enact the regulations needed or useful in the diocese. There is nothing which will excuse entirely from that obligation. If there are extraordinary circumstances which prevent the holding of the synod every ten years, as the Code prescribes, the Holy See should be consulted.[2]

2. *In Dioceses Subject to the Same Bishop*

The second paragraph of canon 356 allows, under certain conditions, a relaxation of the law urged in the first part of the canon. A bishop who is ruling more than one diocese at a time is not strictly obliged to hold a synod in each diocese, but is permitted to convoke to one synod the clergy from both dioceses who should attend their respective synods. There are, however, certain conditions which must be present before this concession can be enjoyed; namely, that

[1] C. 5. Cf. Wernz-Vidal, *De Personis*, p. 670, n. 30; Chelodi, *Jus de Personis*, p. 397.

[2] Vito, *Il Sinodo Diocesano*, p. 11.

either the bishop rules dioceses which are united *aeque principaliter* or that he has one diocese *in titulum* and the perpetual administration of the other.

The Code [3] gives a definition of an equally principal union of benefices. It exists when two or more are so united that they remain as they are and one is not subject to another. Both retain their autonomy, all their titles and rank as though the union had not been made. "It is rather a subjective union because the only change effected by the union is that instead of having distinct rectors the one person rules both without the one benefice being subject to the other." [4] This same terminology, undoubtedly, must be used in reference to the union of dioceses. The type of union in a particular instance, whether it be *aeque principalis* or *minus principalis* (that is, one subject to the other), can be determined only by the words of the constitution which decreed the union.[5] The sense of this concession is, then, that even though two dioceses are united *aeque principaliter* the bishop who rules them is obliged to hold only one synod. He has such a right by common law.[6] Nothing is said in this canon about what is to be done if two dioceses are united *minus principaliter.* But it would seem that only one synod would be necessary, and it would be, according to the principle of canon 1419 § 3 "*accessorium subjicitur principali,*" in the principal diocese because by the very nature of the union one diocese is subject to the other. However if the decree of union ordained otherwise, it must be followed.[7]

The second mitigation of the principle of paragraph § 1 is

[3] C. 1419.

[4] Golden, *Parochial Benefices in the New Code*, p. 24.

[5] Cf. e.g., const. "*Unigenitus*" Benedict XIV, 26 Nov. 1749—*Fontes*, n. 403; Const. Benedict XV "*Ecclesiae Universae,*" 20 Aug. 1921—*A. A. S.*, 1921 (XIII) 467-469.

[6] Previous to the Code, because of several particular decisions of the Congregation of the Council (Cf. Pallotini, *Collectio Omnium Conclusionum et Resolutionum S. C. Concilii*, XVI, 595-598), several authors maintained this opinion. Cf. Benedict XIV, *De Synodo Dioecesana*, l. I, c. 8, n. 4; Phillips, *Compendium Juris Ecclesiastici*, p. 337; Cappello, *De Visitatione Liminum*, I, 305.

[7] Cf. Toso, *Commentaria Minora*, III, 187.

granted to a residential bishop who has a title (*jus in re*) to one diocese and is made the perpetual administrator of another diocese with complete charge of its government but without the personal title of a residential bishop. In this instance the bishop not only has the right to convoke a synod for the diocese of which he is administrator, since according to canon 315 § 1 he has the rights of a residential bishop, but he need hold only one synod for both dioceses. The same faculty, however, is not granted by the Code to one who temporarily administer another diocese, because he is tacitly excluded in the paragraph, but more so because he has only the rights of a Vicar Capitular and, therefore, no power to hold the synod.[8] Only when he is given the right expressly in the letters of his nomination can he exercise such jurisdiction.

All commentators [9] on the Code agree that the second paragraph of canon 356 does not take away from the bishop the power to convoke distinct synods for each diocese if he wishes. It is rather only a special concession freeing from the usual obligation of holding a synod in each diocese, and therefore as a right may or may not be used. If there is good reason to hold a distinct synod, a bishop is perfectly free not to take advantage of this concession. Indeed at times equity and prudence will suggest this as necessary in order to avoid discord and to foster harmony particularly when the people of the dioceses concerned are of a different race or language.[10] It would not seem, however, that a legal custom prescribing distinct synods would continue in force after the Code. For the second paragraph of this canon is a permissive law.[11] Therefore a custom demanding separate synods must be considered as contrary to the canon since it would nullify the right granted by the Code to hold only one synod. According to canon 5, consequently, the custom is abrogated and could be tolerated by the bishop only if it were

[8] Cf. c. 315 § 2 1° taken with c. 357 § 1.

[9] Wernz-Vidal, *De Personis*, p. 668; Toso, *Commentaria Minora*, III, 187; Chelodi, *De Personis*, p. 398, note 2; Coronata, *Institutiones Juris Canonici*, I, 475; Pistocchi, *De Synodo Dioecesana*, p. 20; Vito, *Il Sinodo Diocesano*, p. 15.

[10] Cf. Benedict XIV, *De Synodo Dioecesana*, l. I, c. 5, n. 4.

[11] Cf. Michiels, *Normae Generales*, I, 252-256.

centenary or immemorial and could not be prudently disregarded.

If a bishop has the right to hold one synod for the dioceses which he rules and intends to make use of this concession, it is clear that the clergy of both dioceses have a right to be present. For, even though there is only one synod for all, it is to be considered by a fiction of law the synod of each diocese, and therefore there should be present the representation of the clergy that the Code demands for each synod. Moreover, if the bishop deems it advisable, he may invite more of the clergy to attend. These in their turn are obliged to be present, according to what will be explained in the following chapter, and in the case of contumacy can be constrained by congruent penalties.[12] The laws made in the synod can be in reference to the conditions in either diocese. But it is advisable that the legislation for each diocese be prepared by commissions from that diocese and discussed in distinct preparatory sessions by the clergy concerned. They are the ones who understand the prevailing conditions. Likewise it would be better if separate statutes were formulated. All the legislation, however, may be promulgated together in the synod.[13]

3. *In an Abbey or Prelature Nullius*

According to canon 215 §2: "In jure nomine dioecesis venit quoque abbatia vel praelatura nullius." It is necessary, therefore, in the interpretation of canon 356 §1, to consider briefly the obligation of celebrating a synod in both the abbey and prelature *nullius*.

An abbey or prelature *nullius* may be defined as a territory with clergy and people which is distinct and separated from the jurisdiction of every diocese,[14] and in charge of a prelate who has complete jurisdiction to the exclusion of any bishop. However, it is more than just an exempt territory of a diocese which always remains in the territory of a diocese. It is, as its name indicates, "*nullius dioecesis.*" As Fagnanus expresses it: [15] "It is not made

[12] Cf. cc. 358 §1, §2, 359 §2. Cf. Vito, *Il Sinodo Diocesano*, p. 15.

[13] Cf. Pistocchi, *De Synodo Dioecesana*, pp. 20-21; Vito, *Il Sinodo Diocesano*, p. 16.

[14] C. 319 §1. Cf. Benedict XIV, *De Synodo Dioecesana*, 1. II, c. 11, n. 4; *Dictionnaire de Droit Canonique*, v. Abbaye Nullius, I.

[15] *Commentarium in Libros Decretalium*, 1. I, c. XIX, n. 10.

by simple exemption from diocesan jurisdiction, but through the dismembering of a territory placed in the power of an inferior prelate who has entire jurisdiction over the clergy and the people to the exclusion of the bishop." Whether it is an abbey *nullius* or a prelature *nullius* depends on whether its ruler is an abbot or some other inferior prelate.

Previous to the Code there was no obligation to hold a synod in an abbey or prelature *nullius*. In fact authors [16] declared that one in charge of the territory did not have the right to hold the synod, unless there was a special Apostolic indult to that effect, and besides it could be shown that this had been the practice for some time. Unless these conditions were present all the clergy in the care of souls, as well as the abbot or prelate, were obliged to attend the synod of the bishop who had the right of visitation in the territory. But the Code has not only given the abbot or prelate the right to have their own synod; it has also imposed the obligation of celebrating the synod every ten years the same as every diocese. Baucher [17] states that the Code is silent on this matter, but gives no explanation for his position. Certainly canon 215 §2 implies that the synod is obligatory in the abbey or prelature *nullius* as it is in every diocese.[18] The only exception will be if the territory has not at least three canonically established parishes. In such a case the territory is governed by special laws given by the Holy See, and therefore is not obliged by the Code to celebrate the synod.[19]

4. *In a Vicariate Apostolic*

Previous to the Code there could be no question of any obligation existing to celebrate the synod in a vicariate apostolic. However, Benedict XIV [20] believed a vicar apostolic in missionary lands

[16] Benedict XIV, *De Synodo Dioecesana*, 1. II, c. 11, n. 1-5; 1. III, c. 5, n. 3; Fagnanus, *l. c.;* Ferraris, *Bibliotheca Canonica, Juridica, etc.*, v. Synodus Dioecesana, p. 12; Wernz, *Jus Decretalium*, II b, 734; Cappello, *De Visitatione Liminum*, I, 307; Ojetti, *Synopsis Rerum Moralium et Juris Pontificii*, n. 3898.

[17] *Dictionnaire de Droit Canonique*, v. Abbaye Nullius, V.

[18] Cf. *A. A. S.*, XIII (1921), 291.

[19] C. 319 §2.

[20] *De Synodo Dioecesana*, 1. II, c. 10, n. 8.

had this right. According to the Code, the synod is to be celebrated in the vicariate, though there is no determined time within which this is to be done. Canon 304 §2 states: ". . . quae de Synodo dioecesana can. 356-362, Synodo vicariatus apostolici (praescribuntur); sed nullum est praefinitum tempus pro . . . Synodi celebratione . . ." Cappello [21] denies that any obligation exists and insists that in the place of the synod the annual gatherings, mentioned in canon 303, of at least the principal missionaries can enact whatever regulations are needed. But according to the Code these gatherings do not seem to be intended as a substitute for the synod. They are apparently intended to supplement the work of the synod, since its frequency will have to depend on the varying local conditions. Consequently, even though the time of the synod is not definitely stated, the Code clearly prescribes that the synod be celebrated at some time in the vicariate and practically all authors admit such an obligation.[22] With regard to the time, certainly there is no need under any circumstances to have the synod oftener than every ten years. On the other hand, if conditions are not unfavorable, it cannot be neglected entirely.[23] The most that can be said is that it is up to the prudent judgment of the vicar to determine just when it is needed.

Article II. Right of Convocation

Though the celebration of the synod is imposed as an obligation, it nevertheless supposes that the one who convokes it has the power of jurisdiction to summon the clergy and especially to give legal force to the synodal enactments. It is necessary, therefore, to determine those who have the required jurisdiction and at the same time are not forbidden by the Code to exercise it.

[21] *Summa Juris Canonici,* I, 356.

[22] De Meester, *Compendium Juris Canonici,* II, 122; Chelodi, *Jus de Personis,* p. 398; Vermeersch-Creusen, *Epitome,* I, 231; Vito, *Il Sinodo Diocesano,* p. 21; Winslow, *Vicars and Prefects Apostolic,* pp. 51-53; Vromant, *Jus Missionariorum,* p. 174. Wernz-Vidal (*De Personis,* II, 668) admits that this obligation exists, but maintains it is not strict because there is no time limit.

[23] Vito, *Il Sinodo Diocesano,* p. 22.

1. *The Residential Bishop*

The one who before all others has the right to hold the synod is the bishop of the diocese.[24] Ever since the law prescribing the synod had been enacted, it was implied that the bishop was the one to attend to its convocation; therefore the Code in canon 357 §1 has clearly set forth his right. It is part of the bishop's ordinary jurisdiction which he can exercise without the consent of the Metropolitan or even special permission of the Holy See.[25] In fact the Code makes no mention even of the need of seeking the advice of the cathedral chapter or board of consultors before deciding to hold the synod.[26] However, here in the United States, because the Third Plenary Council of Baltimore has so ordained,[27] bishops are obliged to seek the advice of their diocesan consultors before they convoke the synod.[28] This particular legislation is certainly *beside* the Code. Therefore it continues in force. Despite the fact that the Code is conceding to the bishop the exclusive power to convoke the synod, it does not by that fact imply that the bishop need not seek the advice of the consultors about the convocation of the synod in case that this consultation is demanded by particular law.

The right of the bishop to convoke the synod does not depend on his consecration, since it is due to his power of jurisdiction and not his power of orders. Before the Code authors [29] all agreed that

[24] This, of course, does not include a titular bishop. Cf. c. 348 §1.

[25] Cf. Benedict XIV, *De Synodo Dioecesana,* 1. II, c. 5, n. 1.

[26] This was admitted by authors before the Code. Cf. Benedict XIV, *De Synodo Dioecesana,* 1. XIII, c. 1, n. 13-14; Ferraris, *Bibliotheca Canonica, Juridica, etc.,* v. Synodus Dioecesana, n. 17. The latter author, however, declared that a few held the contrary opinion and the S. C. of the Council (*Calaritana* 16 July 1599—*Fontes,* n. 2327) admitted the value of a contrary custom.

[27] "Ad consultorum attributiones quod pertinet Patres de his convenerunt: (1) *Consilium consultorum exquiret Episcopus pro synodo dioecesana indicenda et publicanda . . .*"—*Acta et Decreta Concilii Plenarii Baltimorensis* III, n. 20.

[28] Klekotka, *Diocesan Consultors,* pp. 112-116.

[29] Barbosa, *De Officio et Potestate Episcopi,* II, 395; Benedict XIV, *De Synodo Dioecesana,* 1. II, c. 5, n. 4-7; Ferraris, *Bibliotheca Canonica, Juridica, etc.,* v. Synodus Dioecesana, n. 7; Bouix, *De Episcopo,* II, 356; Craisson,

a bishop had the power to convoke the synod once his election was confirmed by the Pope and the letters of nomination had been received. But more than canonical institution by the Pope and the reception of the apostolic letters is required by the law of the Code before a bishop has the power of jurisdiction and therefore the right to convoke the synod. The bishop must take canonical possession of the diocese, and if the synod is held before this ceremony is carried out, it would be invalid and any legislation would be null and void.[30] Canonical possession, which may be made even before the ceremony of consecration, is taken by presenting personally or by proxy the apostolic letters of nomination to the cathedral chapter or board of consultors in the presence of the secretary of the chapter or the chancellor, who will record all the proceedings in writing. The bishop is free any time after this ceremony to convoke the synod. With regard to an archbishop, the question has been raised as to whether he may convoke his own diocesan synod before he has received the pallium. Barbosa,[31] Ferraris,[32] Bouix,[33] and Cappello [34] maintained that the previous reception of the pallium was necessary before the archbishop could hold the synod. Wernz [35] denied this, however, because its use was forbidden at the Solemn Mass of the synod.[36] The Code in canon 276 seems clear on the point. Before the reception of the pallium all acts are forbidden, as illicit but not invalid, either of metropolitan jurisdiction or of the episcopal order which, according to the liturgical books, require the use of the pal-

Manuale Totius Juris Canonici, I, 940; Smith, *Elements of Ecclesiastical Law,* I, 292; Aichner, *Compendium Juris Ecclesiastici,* p. 540; Wernz, *Jus Decretalium,* II b, 733.

[30] Cc. 334 §2, 3; 427. Cf. Vermeersch-Creusen, *Epitome,* I, 242.

[31] *De Officio et Potestate Episcopi,* II, 395.

[32] *Bibliotheca Canonica, Juridica, etc.,* v. Synodus Dioec., n. 8.

[33] *De Episcopo,* II, 356.

[34] *De Visitatione Liminum,* I, 306.

[35] *Jus Decretalium,* II b, 733.

[36] Cf. Benedict XIV, *De Synodo Dioecesana,* 1. III, c. 11, n. 7. The passages of this work (1. II, c. 5, n. 8; c. 6, n. 4) usually referred to as authority for the first opinion are concerned only with the necessity of the archbishop having the pallium before convoking the provincial council.

lium.[37] Nothing is said about acts of episcopal jurisdiction; and accordingly authors [38] conclude that the right to convoke the synod certainly belongs to the archbishop even before the reception of the pallium.

The right of the residential bishop to convoke the synod, of course, cannot destroy the power of the Pope by his own immediate ordinary jurisdiction to have the synod celebrated in any diocese. Apparently, too, the competent Roman Congregations, either the Consistorial Congregation or the Congregation of Propaganda, could by reason of their obligation to procure the observance of the common law have the synod celebrated in case a bishop failed to do so.[39] It is certain, however, because of canon 274, that the archbishop has not the power to interfere in any of his suffragan dioceses in regard to this matter.

2. *Abbot or Prelate Nullius*

As has already been noted, it was generally accepted by authors previously to the Code that an abbot or prelate *nullius* had the right to convoke the synod in his own territory only when the power was granted by a special indult of the Holy See and could be proved as a long existing practice. Otherwise he and his clergy had to attend the synod of the bishop who had the right of visitation in that territory.[40]

This has been changed by the Code. Both from the words of canon 215 §2: ". . . et nomine Episcopi [venit quoque], Abbas vel Praelatus *nullius,* nisi ex natura rei vel sermonis contextu aliud con-

[37] Cf. *Pontificale Romanum,* I, de Pallio; *Caeremoniale Episcoporum,* 1. I, c. 16, n. 4; Trombetta, *De Pallio Archiepiscopali,* p. 27.

[38] Wernz-Vidal, *De Personis,* p. 667; Chelodi, *Jus de Personis,* p. 398, note 1; Vito, *Il Sinodo Diocesano,* pp. 19-20; Ayrinhac, *Constitution of the Church,* p. 197; Augustine, *Commentary on Canon Law,* II, 386. However, Pistocchi (*De Synodo Dioecesana,* p. 22) maintains the contrary opinion.

[39] Cf. cc. 248, 252; const. "*Sapienti Consilio,*" Pius X, 29 June 1908, I, 5, 6—*A. A. S.,* I (1909), 9-10, 12-13; Cappello, *De Curia Romana,* I, 111-112, 233-234; Monin, *De Curia Romana,* pp. 198 ff., 239, 281.

[40] This teaching was based on several decisions of the Congregation of the Council: S. C. C. *Nullius,* 17 Aug. 1626—Richter, *Canones et Decreta Conc. Tridentini,* p. 328; S. C. C. *Nullius s. Messan.,* 5 July 1738—*Thesaurus Resolutionum S. C. Concilii ad annum 1738,* p. 106.

stet," and from the fact that the celebration of the synod is now obligatory in an abbey or prelature *nullius,* it is clear that canon 357 §1 must be interpreted as giving the abbot or prelate *nullius* the right to hold his own synod in his territory, once he has taken possession of that territory. This deduction is confirmed by canon 323 §1, which gives the abbot or prelate *nullius* all the ordinary powers of a residential bishop. Moreover, it would seem that the same right to hold a synod has also been conceded to an abbot or prelate who rules a territory without three canonical parishes even though there is not an obligation to have the synod. For there is no reason why such an abbot or prelate cannot be considered as having the usual powers and rights since the Code gives to all abbots and prelates *nullius,* without any restriction, the ordinary faculties of a bishop. Whatever restriction is imposed by canon 319 §2 refers solely to the obligations imposed on the territory and not to the rights of the one who rules it. It, therefore, seems probable that in such a case the abbot or prelate, though not being obliged to hold the synod, can if he wishes celebrate it, unless of course the special law given the territory by the Holy See makes some contrary provision.

3. *Vicars and Prefects Apostolic*

Except for Benedict XIV [41] who admitted the right of convocation, pre-Code authors did not consider the power of the vicars apostolic to hold a synod in their territory. There can be no doubt about the law of the Code in this matter. It follows necessarily from the obligation of holding the synod in the vicariate, as prescribed by canon 304 §2, and it is implicitly reaffirmed by canon 294 §1, which gives to vicars apostolic all the rights of residential bishops. Accordingly authors [42] insist that once the vicar has been named by the Holy See and has taken possession of his territory according to canon 293 §2, he may hold the synod. These same authors, with

[41] *De Synodo Dioecesana,* 1. II, c. 10, n. 2-8.

[42] Winslow, *Vicars and Prefects Apostolic,* p. 51; Wernz-Vidal, *De Personis,* p. 668; Chelodi, *Jus de Personis,* p. 398; Toso, *Commentaria Minora,* III, 188; Vito, *Il Sinodo Diocesano,* pp. 21-22; Vromant, *Jus Missionariorum,* II, 174; Cappello, *Summa Juris Canonici,* I, 356; Vermeersch, *Periodica de re canonica et morali,* IX, 32.

the exception of Chelodi and Cappello who deny it, maintain, moreover, that a prefect apostolic while not being obliged to hold the synod can convoke one if he believes conditions warrant it. Apparently this conclusion must be admitted as a consequence of canon 294 §1, which gives even the prefect apostolic the powers of a residential bishop. There is no reason why the convocation of the synod can be excluded from this general concession.

4. *Administrators Apostolic*

It was commonly accepted before the Code that an administrator apostolic had the power to hold the synod [43] as part of the jurisdiction of his office. Benedict XIV,[44] however, distinguished between the administrator who was appointed to take the place of a bishop unable to rule his diocese and one sent to administer a vacant diocese. In the former instance, Benedict XIV maintained, the synod could not be held without special permission of the Holy See unless the letters of his nomination expressly contained this faculty. In the latter case, however, the administrator could hold the synod as a vicar capitular was able to do.

Basing their interpretation on canon 315 of the Code, present day canonists [45] make a distinction between those appointed to administer a diocese permanently and those appointed only for a time. The former, having all the rights of a residential bishop, are able to celebrate the synod, once they have taken canonical possession of their office. This is confirmed by the prescriptions of canon 356 §2, which gives one who is bishop of one diocese and the perpetual administrator of another the power to hold the one synod for the two dioceses. On the other hand, the latter have no right to convoke the

[43] Ferraris, *Bibliotheca Canonica, etc.*, v. Synodus Dioec., n. 14; Phillips, *Compendium Juris Ecclesiastici*, p. 337; Smith, *Elements of Ecclesiastical Law*, p. 292; Wernz, *Jus Decretalium*, II b, 734; Bouix, *De Episcopo*, II, 357; Cappello, *De Visitatione Liminum*, I, 307. However, Craisson (*Manuale Totius Juris Canonici*, n. 940) declared a special indult of the Holy See was required.

[44] *De Synodo Dioecesana*, 1. II, c. 10, n. 10. Cf. also De Brabandere, *Juris Canonici Compendium*, I, 286.

[45] Wernz-Vidal, *De Personis*, p. 668; Toso, *Commentaria Minora*, III, 188; Pistocchi, *De Synodo Dioecesana*, p. 22.

synod since they enjoy only the powers of the Vicar Capitular, who under the present law cannot validly convoke the synod.[46] The temporary administrator will possess this faculty only when it is expressly granted in his letter of deputation.[47]

5. *Coadjutor Bishop*

Toso [48] denies that a coadjutor bishop, who according to canon 350 §2 is given to the see or to the person of the bishop with the right of succession, can convoke the synod unless this faculty is expressly granted in his letters of deputation. But it would seem that a distinction must be made. It is true that a coadjutor given to the see or one given to the person of a bishop who is not incapacitated has only the rights granted by the letters of his nomination and the express concession of the bishop.[49] However the Code in canon 351 §2 explicitly grants to a coadjutor given to a bishop who is totally incapacitated all the rights of the episcopal office. Therefore it appears that by reason of this general concession such a coadjutor has the right to hold the synod after he has taken canonical possession of his office.

6. *Pro-Vicars and Pro-Prefects Apostolic*

The final class of prelates whose right it is *ex jure* to hold the synod are pro-vicars and pro-prefects who must be appointed in vicariates and prefectures in order that they may assume the care of the territories in the case of the death of the vicar or prefect, or his inability to exercise his jurisdiction. While the vicar or prefect is able to rule the territory the pro-vicar or pro-prefect has no power but what is expressly granted him. However when the vicar or prefect dies or cannot exercise his jurisdiction, the pro-vicar or pro-prefect, as the case may be, immediately assumes *the entire government* of the territory and continues in it until the Holy See fills the vacancy.[50] In other words they are to act as administrators. How-

[46] Cc. 357, §1, 435 §1.

[47] C. 314.

[48] *Commentaria Minora,* III, 188.

[49] Cc. 351 §1, §2, 352. Cf. Wernz-Vidal, *De Personis,* pp. 661-662; Vromant, *Jus Missionariorum,* II, 176.

[50] Cc. 309, 310. Cf. Winslow, *Vicars and Prefects Apostolic,* p. 65 ff.

ever, unlike a temporary apostolic administrator, according to canon 310 §2 they have all the faculties of the vicar or prefect. Therefore during the interim of the vacancy they have the right to call the synod as the vicar or prefect could do. Vromant [51] because of the words of canon 304 §2 ". . . congrua congruis referendo . . ." denies this right of the pro-vicar and pro-prefect. He evidently believes they have only the same powers as a vicar capitular. But the Code in assigning them the entire government of the territory and all the ordinary faculties of vicars or prefects concedes the rights of a residential bishop rather than of the vicar capitular. At least the wording of these canons is a sufficient basis for a solidly probable opinion.

7. *Vicar General*

Though regularly the jurisdiction of the vicar general is the same as belongs to the bishop by law unless the bishop reserves some of these matters to himself, the Code states that certain acts of jurisdiction because of their particular importance cannot be exercised by the vicar general without a special mandate from the bishop.[52] One of these, according to canon 357 §1, is the convocation of the synod. The vicar general is forbidden to exercise this act of jurisdiction without the special authorization of the bishop; and, if he does attempt to do it, according to canon 368 §1 it would appear that the synod is null and void. However, that of itself would not make all the legislation void, although it cannot be considered synodal; for it would not deprive the vicar general of his regular ordinary jurisdiction.

The need of a special mandate applies also to the vicar general of an abbey or prelature ***nullius*** [53] as well as to the vicar delegate of vicariates and prefectures apostolic.[54] Apparently there is only one exception, and that is the right of the Cardinal Vicar of Rome to

[51] *Jus Missionariorum*, II, 176, note 2.

[52] C. 368 §1.

[53] C. 323 §3 taken with c. 368 §1.

[54] Cf. S. C. de Prop., 8 Dec. 1919—*A. A. S.*, XII (1920) 120; Winslow, *Vicars and Prefects Apostolic*, pp. 66-70.

convoke the synod without a special mandate from the Pope because of the broad powers given him.[55]

In connection with this special mandate it is not necessary for its validity that it be given in writing, since the Code makes no such requirement, as it does for many other matters.[56] But as Campagna [57] suggests, this is preferable. The special mandate for the synod may be given in a particular case, or it may be included in a general authorization for all the cases demanded by the Code.[58] In both instances the vicar general will be able to hold the synod. In the event that the mandate is to include the necessary authorization for all the cases requiring a special mandate it is disputed whether this may be expressed in a formula as: "etiam quoad omnia quae speciale mandatum requirunt" or whether specific mention must be made of the particular acts as enumerated in the Code.[59] Since both opinions are probable, either may be followed in practice.

8. *Vicar Capitular or Administrator*

The inability of the Vicar Capitular, and by reason of canon 431 §2 the Administrator of a vacant diocese without a cathedral chapter, to convoke the synod is a restriction imposed by the Code which before was not in force. Previously authors agreed that the vicar capitular had this power and that the chapter could not reserve this to itself to be exercised only with a special mandate. There was, however, a difference of opinion as to when the vicar capitular could exercise it. Some [60] maintained that a year from the last synod had to elapse before the synod could be convoked. This was in accord

[55] Benedict XIV, *De Synodo Dioecesana,* l. II, c. 3, n. 3; Ferraris, *Bibliotheca Canonica, Juridica, etc.,* v. Synodus Dioecesana, n. 9; Wernz, *Jus Decretalium,* II b, 734.

[56] Cf. e. g., cc. 364 §1, 465 §4, 497 §1, §3.

[57] *Il Vicario Generale del Vescovo,* p. 131.

[58] Campagna, *o. c.,* pp. 131-132.

[59] Cf. Campagna, *l. c.,* and the authors referred to there.

[60] Barbosa, *De Officio et Potestate Episcopi,* II, 395; Benedict XIV, *De Synodo Dioecesana,* l. II, c. 9, n. 4-6; De Brabandere, *Juris Canonici Compendium,* I, 286; Aichner, *Compendium Juris Ecclesiastici,* p. 450; Wernz, *Jus Decretalium,* II b, 734; Ojetti, *Synopsis Rerum Moralium et Juris Pontificii,* n. 3898.

with a decision of the Congregation of the Council.[61] Other authors [62] did not, however, require this lapse of time and insisted that the synod could be convoked by the vicar capitular immediately upon his entrance into office.

The Code in canon 357 §1 explicitly denies the right of the vicar capitular to hold the synod. Moreover, because canon 435 §1 states that the vicar capitular does not receive jurisdiction for what is forbidden by the law, if the synod is convoked it is null. It would not seem, however, that any legislation there enacted would be void. This prohibition not to hold the synod does not destroy the broad powers of the vicar capitular given to him by canon 435 §1 unless perhaps what was enacted was in violation of canon 436: "Sede vacante nihil innovetur." The reason for this change in the Code is clear. Since the synod need now be held only every ten years the short time longer in which the see is vacant, as is usually the case, will not as a rule make the synod imperative, even if the former bishop had not held the synod at the prescribed time. However, if in an exceptional case the vicar capitular or the administrator deem it necessary to convoke the synod, or want permission to preside over a synod convoked by the former bishop, it would be proper for them to apply to the Holy See for the necessary power.[63] This same restriction applies also to the vicar capitular of an abbey or prelature *nullius;* [64] but, as has already been noted, apparently not to a pro-vicar or pro-prefect during the vacancy of the vicariate or prefecture apostolic.

Article III. Frequency of the Synod

The prescription of canon 356 §1 concerning the frequency of the synod is one of the important changes which have been made in the

[61] S. C. Conc., 13 Sept. 1721—*Fontes,* n. 3232.

[62] Ferraris, *Bibliotheca Canonica, etc.,* v. Synodus Dioecesana, n. 11; Phillips, *Compendium Juris Ecclesiastici,* p. 336; Smith, *Elements of Ecclesiastical Law,* I, 292; Cappello, *De Visitatione Liminum,* I, 306-309. Gousset (*Exposition des Principes du Droit Canonique,* p. 317) also maintained this opinion but insisted that it could be followed only if the diocese was expected to be vacant for a time.

[63] Pistocchi, *De Synodo Dioecesana,* p. 23.

[64] C. 327 §1.

present legislation in order to bring the requirements concerning the diocesan synod into accord with present conditions. This change was the result of a gradual development of opinion. As has already been indicated, suggestions had been made at the Council of Trent to have the synod less frequently than once each year,[65] in order that its celebration would be easier. But no change was made at the time. With this same purpose in view legislation was drafted in the Vatican Council which decreed that the synod be held every three years.[66] Accordingly it was to be expected that the Code would make some change in this matter. The first schema of the Code sent to the various Ordinaries contained a canon prescribing the celebration of the synod every six years. But even this was amplified and the law now orders the synod to be held at least every ten years. Augustine [67] maintains that the period of ten years is to be reckoned from the date the Code went into effect. Since the obligation to hold the synod existed in the pre-Code legislation, the change of its frequency from one year to at least ten years that became effective in the Code must be interpreted in connection with the previous law. Consequently the date from which the extended time must be computed should be that from which the previous obligation was computed; that is, the date of the last synod in the diocese. The change in the frequency of the synod might be the occasion of some surprise. But as Ayrinhac [68] points out, "bishops have now in pastoral retreats, ecclesiastical conferences, and other clerical gatherings frequent opportunities to meet their priests, give them instructions, correct possible abuses, and promote piety and study among them; synods have become less needed than in the past."

Authors [69] agree that the words ". . . decimo saltem quoque anno . . ." do not deprive a bishop of the right to celebrate the synod more frequently if he wishes. Nor would such an ordinance, if en-

[65] *Conc. Tridentini Diariorum . . . Nova Collectio,* IX, 825-26, 864.

[66] "Schema constitutionis de episcopis, de synodis et de vicariis generalibus" —Mansi, LIII, 721.

[67] *Commentary on Canon Law,* II, 385.

[68] *Constitution of the Church,* p. 196.

[69] Wernz-Vidal, *De Personis,* p. 670; Blat, *Commentarium Codicis,* II, 325; Pistocchi, *De Synodo Dioecesana,* p. 13; Vito, *Il Sinodo Diocesano,* p. 11; *Le Canoniste Contemporain,* XLVI (1924), 260.

acted in a plenary or provincial council, be contrary to the law of the Code. What is prescribed is that not more than ten years should elapse between two synods of a diocese. There are circumstances as, for example, persecution, social revolution, or the like, which might make it impossible to have the synod at the required time. If such a case arises, the bishop should provide as best he can some means to supply the place of the synod and thus give the clergy and people the guidance that is necessary particularly in such circumstances. Vito [70] suggests either a diocesan bulletin, special spiritual exercises for the clergy and people, or an annual meeting of priests of certain sections in the presence of the bishop accordingly as is feasible. Besides it would be advisable to inform the Holy See of the circumstances and obtain its directions, unless the time for the quinquennial report is at hand when information about the synod must be given.[71]

Article IV. Place of the Synod

It is indeed proper, as Benedict XIV [72] points out, that the synod, which is a public and solemn act of episcopal jurisdiction, should be celebrated in the cathedral church, "the mother and head of all the churches in the diocese" and the church to which the bishop is especially bound. Accordingly canon 357 §1 prescribes that regularly the synod is to be held in the cathedral. But this need be understood only of the solemn sessions. It is permissible to have the preparatory sessions in any convenient place.[73] If there is a special reason, however, the Code permits the synod to be celebrated elsewhere in the diocese; for the jurisdiction of the bishop can in no way depend on the place where the synod takes place.[74] Thus for example, for the sake of the possible accommodations for the clergy, the synod can be held in the diocesan seminary, as is the

[70] *Il Sinodo Diocesano*, p. 14.

[71] S. Consist. Cong., 4 Nov. 1918, *De Relationibus Dioecesanis*, c. iv, n. 34—*A. A. S.*, X (1918), 493.

[72] *De Synodo Dioecesana*, 1. I, c. 5, n. 5-6.

[73] Ojetti, *Synopsis Rerum Moralium et Juris Pontificii*, n. 3901.

[74] C. 358 §1 6° presupposes that the bishop may hold the synod outside the episcopal city. Cf. Blat, *Commentarium Codicis*, II, 328; Vito, *Il Sinodo Diocesano*, p. 27.

practice in many dioceses. But, whatever place is chosen, it should be a church since the Pontificale Romanum [75] and the *Caeremoniale Episcoporum* [76] suppose that as the place for the synod. It is even permitted in the case of expulsion, persecution, disease and the like to hold the synod outside the diocese, as long as the Ordinary of the place gives his permission.[77]

In the case where a bishop celebrates, according to canon 356 §2, one synod for two dioceses, he has the right to hold it in either of the two. But prudence will often demand that the synod be held alternately in one diocese and then the other in order to avoid the beginnings of any discord. Moreover, a bishop will be bound to do this if a legitimate custom exists in favor of this practice. There is no need even that such a custom be centenary or immemorial, as Pistocchi [78] and Vito [79] maintain. For a custom of this sort is not contrary to the law of the Code which allows a bishop to hold one synod for several dioceses but is silent about in which diocese it is to be celebrated.

[75] III, 5—*Ordo ad Synodum.*

[76] 1. I, c. XXXI, n. 1.

[77] Cc. 201 §3, 1637, 20. Cf. Benedict XIV, *De Synodo Dioecesana,* 1. I, c. 5, n. 2.

[78] *De Synodo Dioecesana,* p. 26.

[79] *Il Sinodo Diocesano,* pp. 16-17, note 1.

CHAPTER V

MEMBERSHIP OF THE SYNOD

Canon 358—§ 1. Ad Synodum vocandi sunt ad eamque venire debent:

1.° Vicarius Generalis;

2.° Canonici ecclesiae cathedralis aut consultores dioecesani;

3.° Rector Seminarii dioecesani saltem maioris;

4.° Vicarii foranei;

5.° Deputatus uniuscuiusque collegialis ecclesiae a Capitulo eiusdem ecclesiae e gremio eligendus;

6.° Parochi civitatis in qua Synodus celebratur;

7.° Unus saltem parochus ex unoquoque vicariatu foraneo eligendus ab omnibus qui curam animarum actu inibi habeant; parochus autem electus debet pro tempore absentiae vicarium substitutum sibi sufficere ad normam can. 465, § 4;

8.° Abbates de regimine et unus e Superioribus cuiusque religionis clericalis qui in dioecesi commorentur, designatus a Superiore provinciali, nisi domus provincialis sit in dioecesi et Superior provincialis interesse ipse maluerit.

§ 2. Episcopus, si opportunum iudicaverit, potest ad Synodum vocare alios quoque et etiam omnes canonicos, parochos, Superiores religiosos, imo et singulos suae dioecesis saeculares sacerdotes, iis tamen exceptis qui necessarii sunt ne in paroeciis animarum cura desit; invitati autem ius suffragii in omnibus habent, perinde ac ceteri, nisi Episcopus in invitatione aliud expresse caverit.

Canon 359—§ 1. Iis qui ad Synodum venire debent, si legitimo impedimento detineantur, non licet mittere procuratorem qui eorum nomine Synodo intersit; sed Episcopum de impedimento certiorem faciant.

§ 2. Negligentes Episcopus potest iustis poenis compellere et punire, nisi de religiosis exemptis agatur qui parochi non sunt.

The prescriptions of the Code in regard to the membership of the synod are a change from the former legislation. Previously, all the priests, whether diocesan or religious, who had the care of souls as well as religious who, even though exempt from episcopal jurisdiction, were not subject to a general chapter, were obliged to be present at the synod. Since this requirement was found in so many instances to make the celebration of the synod almost impossible, less stringent regulations in this matter have been made in the Code. Under the present law all that is absolutely necessary is a representation of the body of the clergy, although the bishop may, if he judge it feasible, summon any of the others that he wishes as long as enough remain in the parishes to take care of the needs of the people.

Article I. Prescribed Membership

Canon 358 §1 determines exactly who must be summoned to the synod in order that it be held legitimately: "*Ad Synodum vocandi sunt* . . ." In other words, it states who have the right to be present. Vidal [1] remarks that the former discipline was concerned principally with those who were obliged to come to the synod. Nothing was said about their right to be summoned, although some authors[2] maintained that this was implied. There can be no doubt now about this; the Code is sufficiently clear. A custom which would exclude any of the clergy mentioned in the first paragraph of this canon from being summoned to the synod according to canon 5 has been abrogated by the Code and could be tolerated only if it was immemorial or centenary and could not be prudently disregarded. Moreover, if actually one of these would be excluded from mem-

[1] Wernz-Vidal, *De Personis*, p. 699, note 1.

[2] De Brabandere, *Juris Canonici Compendium*, I, 287; Aichner, *Compendium Juris Ecclesiastici*, p. 450; Claeys-Bouuaert, *De Canonica Cleri Saecularis Obedientia*, p. 85. However, Phillips (*Compendium Juris Ecclesiastici*, p. 337) did not admit this right.

bership, there might be some reason to doubt whether or not the gathering was really a synod. This in turn, while it would not affect the force of the legislation since the bishop alone is the legislator, would raise the question as to whether the officials to be approved in the synod were validly chosen. Vito [3] insists that it is necessary for the validity of the synod that the vicar general be invited, but says nothing about the others. It is difficult, however, to establish the invalidity in any instance by certain proof, and therefore, according to canon 11, in practice the synod must be regarded as valid.

1. *Vicar General*

Before the Code, while admittedly there was no obligation, authors [4] recommended that the vicar general be invited to the synod to assist the bishop in carrying out its work. Under the present law it is obligatory to summon the vicar general once canonical provision of his office has been made. In the event that a diocese has more than one vicar general, as is permitted by canon 366 §3, all of these have the right to be present, since there is no reason why one should be called in preference to the others.[5] Probably, too, one appointed temporarily to this office, in case the ordinary vicar general is absent from the diocese or prevented from exercising his office, would also enjoy the right to be called to the synod.[6] But it would not seem that a retired vicar general, who has been allowed to retain this name as an honorary title,[7] would possess a similar right; for actually he no longer has the office.

Undoubtedly the vicar general of an abbey or prelature *nullius* must be summoned to the synod of his territory.[8] Moreover, because

[3] *Il Sinodo Diocesano*, p. 23.

[4] Benedict XIV, *De Synodo Dioecesana*, l. III, c. 3, n. 2; Gousset, *Exposition des Principes du Droit Canonique*, p. 318; Phillips, *Compendium Juris Ecclesiastici*, p. 337; Wernz, *Jus Decretalium*, II b, 735; Cappello, *De Visitatione Liminum*, I 307.

[5] Cf. Wernz-Vidal, *De Personis*, p. 669; Toso, *Commentaria Minora*, III, 189.

[6] Cf. Campagna, *Il Vicario Generale del Vescovo*, pp. 106-107.

[7] Boudinhon, *Revue du Clergé*, CI (1920), 456 ff.

[8] C. 323 §3.

of the words of canon 304 §2 ". . . congrua congruis referendo," the vicar delegate ought to be called to a synod celebrated in a vicariate or prefecture apostolic. But the Code does not give a similar right to the pro-vicar or pro-prefect even according to the principle of canon 304 §2 since there are not officials similar to pro-vicars and pro-prefects outside vicariates and prefectures apostolic.

2. *Cathedral Chapter or Diocesan Consultors*

The canons of the cathedral church, who according to canon 391 compose the advisory council of the bishop, are the second group that enjoys the right to attend the synod. Certainly it is proper for these to assist at the synod in the framing of the statutes, since they are intended by the Code to have so important a part in the government of the diocese. This fact was recognized before the Code and, although there was no law to that effect, authors [9] regarded this as one of the duties of the chapter. It is to be noted that the Code does not propose simply a right of representation as for collegiate chapters. Hence all the canons of the cathedral chapter have the right to be invited to the synod. The bishop is not permitted to summon only a representation to the synod, in order that divine office will continue as usual during the synod. However as far as possible the synod should not interfere with this duty.[10] Moreover, during the time of the synod, according to canon 420 9°, the canons who are attending the synod are excused from choir and are not to be deprived of the revenues of their prebend or the daily distributions. The right of each canon, whether he has a dignity or a simple canon, will be given when he has taken possession of his office.[11] Honorary canons,[12] however, and even a coadjutor canon will not have the right to be called to the synod unless this has been expressly granted in their letters of appointment.[13]

[9] Barbosa, *De Officio et Potestate Episcopi,* I, 396; Benedict XIV, *De Synodo Dioecesana,* 1. III, c. 4, n. 2.

[10] Pistocchi, *De Synodo Dioecesana,* p. 29; Coronata, *Institutiones Juris Canonici,* I, 476.

[11] Cc. 405, 1443-1445.

[12] C. 407 §2.

[13] Cf. Wernz-Vidal, *De Personis,* p. 711.

In dioceses in which there is no cathedral chapter, the board of consultors appointed to assist in the government of the diocese has the right to be called to the synod.[14] This right will be given to each consultor immediately when canonical provision for the office has been made according to canon 148 §1, that is, upon his appointment by the bishop and the acceptance by the consultor. Apparently, too, because of the words of canon 304 §2 ". . . congrua congruis referendo . . .", the same right has been given to the *consiliarii* to be appointed in vicariates and prefectures apostolic.[15]

3. *Rector of the Major Seminary*

The obligation to summon the rector of the major seminary to the synod is entirely new legislation. The reason for this prescription is clear. It is he who has the care of the future diocesan priests, and therefore he should have a part in the legislative enactments of the synod. Moreover, since according to canon 1368 he is considered as a pastor of the seminary, he should be present at the synod as its representative to explain its needs.

By the words ". . . *saltem maioris* . . ." the Code clearly states that the rector of the major seminary must be called to the synod once he has been appointed to this office and accepted his appointment.[16] But authors [17] agree that there is not an obligation of summoning the rector of the minor seminary to the synod, although certainly the right to do so is implied. Apparently this would be true, as Toso maintains, although Vito denies it, if there were only a minor seminary in the diocese, and no major seminary. The text of the law taken strictly favors this interpretation. Even here in the United States where the Second Plenary Council of Baltimore [18] had prescribed that the rectors of the seminaries attend the synod, there does not appear to be an obligation any longer to summon

[14] Cc. 423, 427.

[15] C. 302. Cf. Vromant, *Jus Missionariorum,* II, 174, 177, n. 3.

[16] C. 148 §1. Cf. Cox, *Administration of Seminaries,* p. 82.

[17] Toso, *Commentaria Minora,* III, 190; Wernz-Vidal, *De Personis,* p. 669; Vito, *Il Sinodo Diocesano,* p. 25.

[18] *Acta et Decreta,* n. 66.

the rector of the minor seminary even if the diocese had no major seminary. The reason is that this legislation seems to be contrary to the law of the Code and hence is abrogated by canon 6 1°. The Code in canon 358 §2 has given the bishop the right to convoke the remaining members of the clergy not mentioned in the first paragraph according as he sees fit. This faculty has been given to the bishop in order to make the celebration of the synod easier than it had been in the past. Consequently particular law cannot nullify the advantage of this concession by obliging the bishop to convoke some of the clergy not mentioned in the first paragraph.

A difficulty arises in the case of a rector of a seminary established by several bishops with the necessary permission of the Holy See to take care of their students for the priesthood.[19] Has the rector of such a seminary the right to attend the synod in the diocese of each of these bishops? The reason one might be inclined to believe that such a right exists is because of a fiction of law admitted on several occasions by the Holy See [20] to the effect that a bishop can regard as his own an inter-diocesan or regional seminary and so has certain rights over it. It might be argued, therefore, that the rector must be regarded by each bishop as his own. However, the words *seminarii dioecesani* apparently have been used as excluding an inter-diocesan seminary as in canon 1354 and therefore implicitly deny such a right. Moreover, as Toso points out, it is not urgent for the bishops to have the rector of an inter-diocesan seminary present at the synods. The Holy See at the time of the erection of the seminary makes special provisions that it will be administered well.[21]

[19] Of course, in the case of a seminary established as diocesan but which admits students from other dioceses which have not concurred in its erection there is no difficulty.

[20] Cf. Const. "*Susceptum inde,*" IV, 25 March 1914—*A. A. S.*, VI (1914), 216; S. C. Conc. July 9, 1921—*A. A. S.*, XVI (1924), 399; Epist., "*Officiorum omnium,*" Aug. 1, 1922—*A. A. S.*, XIV (1922), 456-457; Cox, *Administration of Seminaries*, p. 74.

[21] Cf. Const. "*Susceptum inde,*" V-VIII, 25 March 1914—*A. A. S.*, VI (1914), 216.

4. *Vicars Forane*

The vicars forane of the diocese certainly should be present at the synod if its purpose is to be fully realized. According to canon 445 these officials are entrusted with the different districts of the diocese and have the duty as representatives of the bishop to keep a close vigilance on conditions. They perhaps more than any other can bring to the synod an account of the exact status of the diocese. Their testimony, since it is that of eye-witnesses, is most important.[22] Accordingly, pre-Code authors [23] maintained that even if they were not pastors they should be among the members of the synod. Even when the Holy See granted indults permitting a restriction of the membership required according to the Tridentine law, it nevertheless insisted on the presence of the vicars forane.

The Code prescribes that all the forane vicars of the diocese should be summoned to the synod. This will be their right as long as the canonical provision of their office has been made according to canon 148 §1. In the same way, when a synod is held in a vicariate or prefecture apostolic, quasi-forane vicars and superiors of districts, whom the Holy See [24] wishes to be appointed in vicariates and prefectures apostolic that have only quasi-parishes, will enjoy the right to be convoked to the synod. The reason is the words "congrua congruis referendo" of canon 304 §2.

5. *Representatives of the Collegiate Chapters*

While there is not a similar need for the other chapters of the diocese to assist at the synod as there is for the cathedral chapter, as the advisers of the bishop, it is nevertheless proper that these special groups of the clergy should at least have some representation there. Thus the Code has given to each collegiate chapter as a moral person the right to send a representative to the synod. It is

[22] Cf. Zaplontik, *De Vicariis Foraneis,* p. 130; Pistocchi, *De Synodo Dioecesana,* pp. 30-31.

[23] Cf. Benedict XIV, *De Synodo Dioecesana,* 1. III, c. 3, n. 10; De Brabandere, *Juris Canonici Compendium,* I, 287; Aichner, *Compendium Juris Ecclesiastici,* p. 450; Wernz, *Jus Decretalium,* II b. 735.

[24] Instructio S. C. de Prop. Fide, 25 July 1920, ad 9—*A. A. S.*, XII (1920), 332-333.

to be noted, however, that the Code specifies only one deputy and, therefore, the chapters are not free to send any number they wish.[25] This would be so even if a legitimate custom existed to the contrary, since it would interfere with the permissive law in the second paragraph of this canon by reason of which a bishop is free to convoke others besides the ones mentioned in the first paragraph.

There is no qualification in the Code for the deputy of the chapter other than that he be a member of the chapter, that is, according to canon 393 §2 possessing a dignity or simple canonship. There is, therefore, no need that the one in the highest dignity be chosen nor even the one who is the parochial vicar. The choice of the deputy is to be made according to canon 101 §1 1°, which governs the acts of collegiate moral persons.[26] It is not required, as Augustine [27] and Pistocchi [28] maintain, that the norms of canons 160-178 for canonical elections be followed, since this temporary deputation cannot be considered an ecclesiastical office as defined by canon 145 §1 to which the rules for election apply.[29] The choice of the deputy will be made when an absolute majority of the votes is obtained on the first two ballots or a relative majority on the third. If, however, the third ballot results in a tie, the one who presides will determine the choice of the deputy by his vote. The one selected is excused from choir during the time of synod and in his absence retains the right to the revenue from his prebend and to the daily contributions.[30]

6. *The Pastoral Clergy*

The brief outline of the history of the legislation on the synod shows clearly that from its beginning the pastoral clergy were present. In fact their presence was most necessary, since the supervision of the pastoral work in the diocese has always been the most

25 Blat, *Commentarium Codicis*, II, 327.

26 Blat, *Commentarium Codicis*, II, 328; Toso, *Commentaria Minora*, III, 190; Vito, *Il Sinodo Diocesano*, p. 26.

27 *Rights and Duties of Ordinaries*, p. 94.

28 *De Synodo Dioecesana*, pp. 31-32.

29 Maroto, *Institutiones Juris Canonici*, I, 728.

30 C. 420 §9.

important office of the synod. The Code has retained the traditional notion of the synod as an assembly of the clergy in the care of souls, but at the same time has accommodated its prescriptions to the changed conditions by demanding that only the pastors of the synodal city and a pastor from each deanery be present. In this way a sufficient participation of the pastoral clergy is assured.

A. Pastors of the City of the Synod

Ordinarily, in accord with the prescription of canon 357 §2, the synod should be held in the cathedral, and consequently all the pastors of the episcopal city will have the right to be invited to the synod. But this right is not absolute; it depends on the place of the synod. Therefore, in case a bishop intends to hold the synod in another place in the diocese, the pastors of the cathedral city would no longer have the right to be invited. Instead the pastors of the city or town where the synod is to be celebrated would have to be summoned. Moreover in the event that with the consent of the Ordinary of the place the synod is held outside of the diocese, there would apparently be no obligation for the bishop to invite all the pastors of any city or town of his diocese. It would be sufficient to summon one pastor from each deanery.

This canon, then, gives the right to be present at the synod to all in the city or town of the synod who, according to canon 451 §1, are given a title to a parish with the care of souls under the authority of the Ordinary of the place, after they have been canonically instituted according to canon 455 §1 and have been installed as canons 1443-1445 prescribe. They are to be called to the synod whether they are irremovable or removable pastors, and whether they are of the secular clergy or religious to whom the parish is given as distinct from entrusting the parish to a religious institute.[31] Likewise this same right belongs to quasi-pastors and perhaps even to titulars of mission stations in vicariates and prefectures apostolic by reason of canon 451 §2 1° [32] and the prescrip-

[31] Cf. Vermeersch, "Breve Commentarium in Facultates Legatorum Apostolicorum, n. 8—*Jus Pontificium,* IV (1924), 143-144.

[32] "Parochis aequiparantur cum omnibus iuribus et obligationibus paroecialibus et parochorum nomine in iure veniunt:

1°. Quasi-parochi, qui quasi-paroecias regunt, de quibus in can. 216 §3."

tion ". . . congrua congruis referendo . . ." of canon 304 §2.[33] Undoubtedly, too, parochial vicars with full parochial powers must be invited to the synod, since canon 451 §2 2° states that whatever is said of pastors in the Code is to be understood of them also. Toso[34] denies this because he believes that, since the legislator used the words ". . . omnibus qui curam animarum . . . habeant" in section 7 of this paragraph of canon 358, it was intended that the word *parochi* of this section should be taken as designating pastors strictly so-called. But that term is not enough of itself to indicate that the legislator wished in this instance to restrict the general principle laid down in canon 451 §2 2°. Therefore, after their canonical institution, the vicar who has charge of a parish united to a religious house, or a collegiate church,[35] or any other moral person; the *vicarius oeconomus* or administrator; the adjutant vicar who assumes all the pastoral obligations; the substitute vicar who has not at the time of his appointment had any limitations placed on his rights—all have the right to be called to the synod when it is held in the city or town within the limits of which they have their parish.[36]

B. Representation of the Pastoral Clergy

The Code provides that the clergy in the care of souls outside the city or town of the synod should be represented at the synod by at least one pastor from each deanery who comes as the deputy of the others. More than one representative may be sent; however, this will not depend upon the wish of the clergy but on the permission of the bishop. The Code grants the right of only one to be

[33] Cf. Vromant, *Jus Missionariorum*, II, 177, note 5; 276 ff.

[34] Commentaria Minora, III, 190.

[35] Pistocchi (*De Synodo Dioecesana*, p. 32) and Vito (*Il Sinodo Diocesano*, p. 27) maintain that the parochial vicar of a collegiate chapter in the city where the synod is held has not the right to be present, but only the deputy of the entire chapter. There is not, however, any reason to exclude the parochial vicar from the general term *parochi*, especially since according to canon 471 §4 the pastoral rights which such a vicar enjoys are exclusively his. However, the parochial vicar may come to the synod as the deputy of the chapter.

[36] Cc. 451 §2, 465 §4, 471-475.

present. Moreover, the one chosen must be a pastor. But this is to be understood as above and therefore includes the vicars of a church united to a moral person,[37] administrators of vacant parishes, and substitute and adjutant vicars if they have full parochial power.[38] There is no other requirement explicitly stated in the Code. Probably it is implied that the one chosen should not be the vicar forane, if he is a pastor, since the Code prescribes in separate sections that the vicar forane should come as the head of the deanery and the pastor as a representative of the pastoral clergy.[39] In vicariates and prefectures apostolic the general principle ". . . congrua congruis referendo . . ." will require the deputation of a quasi-pastor or even the titular of a mission station as the representative of each quasi forane vicariate.[40]

Authors,[41] with the exception of Pistocchi[42] who maintains that the norms for canonical elections must be observed, agree that the choice of the pastor who is to represent the deanery at the synod is to be made according to canon 101 §1 1°, which was explained in reference to the selection of a deputy from the collegiate chapters. There is no need to follow the norms of canonical elections, since the act of representing the clergy at the synod is not an ecclesiastical office as defined by canon 145 §1. There is, however, a diversity of opinion as regards who can participate in the selection. Vito[43] and Fanfani[44] maintain that only pastors who have title to a parish, the vicars in charge of a church united to a moral person, and

[37] Pistocchi (*De Synodo Dioecesana*, p. 36) denies this since they are not pastors in the strict sense of the word. However, canon 451 §2 2° gives them all the rights of a pastor.

[38] Vito (*Il Sinodo Diocesano*, p. 30) and Coronata (*Institutiones Juris Canonici*, I 476) exclude the three latter types of vicars from the term *parochi* since they do not receive the parish *in titulum*. But the Code in canon 451 §2 2° makes no such requirements for them to be considered as pastors with full parochial rights.

[39] Vito, *Il Sinodo Diocesano*, p. 29, note 1.

[40] Vromant, *Jus Missionariorum*, p. 177, note 6.

[41] Blat, *Commentarium Codicis*, II, 328; Toso, *Commentaria Minora*, III, 191; Coronata, *Institutiones Juris Canonici*, I, 476.

[42] *De Synodo Dioecesana*, p. 34.

[43] *Il Sinodo Diocesano*, pp. 29-30.

[44] *De Jure Parochorum*, p. 340.

the administrators of vacant parishes may choose the deputy of the deanery. Vermeersch [45] includes besides the clergy already mentioned all the parochial vicars who have full parochial power but denies that assistants (*vicarii cooperatores*), adjutant vicars who have not complete charge of the parish, and substitute vicars whose powers are limited may assist in the selection. Ayrinhac [46] and Toso [47] include all parochial vicars except assistants; while Pistocchi,[48] Magnin,[49] Coronata,[50] and Oesterle [51] consider that even these have the right to express their choice.

The solution of the difficulty lies in the proper interpretation of the clause "qui curam animarum . . . habeant." Vito insists that these words refer only to the clergy who have the primary duty of caring for souls and not to those who temporarily substitute or assist in this work. But no reason can be given to prove that the clause must be understood in such a restricted sense. It is evident that a pastor or even an administrator has not an exclusive obligation in the ministry. Others can be assigned with the general duty of caring for the spiritual welfare of a parish, although the actual exercise of their obligation is to be regulated by the imposed restrictions and the determinations of the pastor. In the same way, while a bishop is the first pastor of the diocese with the antecedent obligation of pastoral care, others assume the work with similar obligation. In fact the Code [52] in referring to all parochial vicars, implies that they have the care of souls. Hence, it is not going beyond the meaning of these words to maintain that all the parochial vicars of each deanery are given the right to participate in the selection of a pastor to act as their representative at the synod. Moreover it would appear that the general clause *qui curam animarum*

[45] *Epitome,* I, 252.

[46] *Constitution of the Church,* p. 119.

[47] *Commentaria Minora,* III, 191

[48] *De Synodo Dioecesana,* p. 34.

[49] *Le Canoniste Contemporain,* XLVI (1924), 264.

[50] *Institutiones Juris Canonici,* I, 476.

[51] *Praelectiones Juris Canonici,* I, 183.

[52] Cc. 474, 475 §2, 476 §1, 7. Cf. also cc. 131 §3, 367 §3 and decision of S. C. Conc. 14 Jan. 1922—*A. A. S.*, XIV (1922), 229 ff. for a distinction between pastors and others having the care of souls.

habeant includes all those in charge of churches or missions which are not yet formed into actual parishes [53] as well as the chaplains of communities and institutions who have been given jurisdiction independent from that of the pastor.[54] In a word, all who have any share whatsoever in the pastoral work have been given the right to be represented at the synod.

Canon 358 §1 7° repeats the provision of canon 465 §4 that arrangement be made for a substitute vicar during the absence of the pastor. According to canon 465 §4, if the pastor is to be absent for more than a week, he should have a substitute who is approved by the Ordinary or, if a religious, by the Ordinary and religious Superior. The question then arises as to whether there is the same obligation if the pastor will be away at the synod, less than a week as will usually be the case. A comparison of canons 358 §1 7° and 465 §4 does not indicate that it is obligatory to appoint a substitute vicar for an absence of less than a week. There is no reason to conclude that this canon on the synod changed the general principle of canon 465 §4. Vito, however, believes that it is obligatory to designate a substitute vicar because canon 358 §1 7° does not make a distinction between the absence of more than a week and less than that. In practice, according to canon 15, there will not be an obligation to appoint a substitute vicar, unless a pastor wishes to devote himself entirely to some special synodal work. However, in any case the pastor will be obliged, by reason of canon 465 §6, to make some provision that the needs of his parishioners will be attended to during the time of his absence regardless of how brief it is.

7. *Religious Superiors*

Instead of retaining the prescriptions of the former law according to which all religious in the care of souls as well as those not engaged in the pastoral work but who were not subject to a general chapter were obliged to attend the synod, the Code now gives the right of membership at the synod only to certain religious superiors who are to represent their subjects.

[53] Cf. S. Cong. Consist., 1 Aug. 1919—*A. A. S.*, XI (1919), 346-347.
[54] C. 464 §2.

All abbots *de regimine*, that is, those who rule an exempt house within the territory of the diocese [55] have the right to be invited to the synod, whether or not their communities are engaged in pastoral work. The essential requirement is that they actually are independent superiors; and, therefore, abbots who are given the title *honoris causa* have not a similar right,[56] nor have those who as delegates have charge of priories dependent on autonomous abbeys.[57] Moreover, abbots *nullius* who rule an exempt house but not in the territory of the diocese are not included, since they are obliged to hold a synod for their own territory.

The Code likewise grants the right of participation in the synod to one superior of each clerical religion in the diocese, whether the institute is an order or a congregation, of pontifical or diocesan right. It is to be noted that the institute must be a clerical religion, which is, according to canon 488 4°, one in which many of the members will be raised to the priesthood. The superior to be chosen to attend the synod, need be only a minor local superior,[58] that is, a superior in charge of a religious house juridically established as a moral person.[59] One in charge of a filial house depending on another house is not eligible. The provincial of the religion whose jurisdiction extends to the houses of that diocese selects the superior who will attend the synod; or, if the houses of the diocese belong to different provinces of the institute, the respective provincials will designate the superior. In case the institute is not divided into provinces, apparently the superior of the whole religion will select a superior to represent the institute at the synod. It is necessary to choose one of the local superiors in the diocese, and in the event that there is only one house it must be the superior of that house. Under no circumstance can more than one superior be sent to the synod unless

[55] Schäfer, *De Religiosis*, p. 271.

[56] Vermeersch-Creusen, *Epitome*, I, 252; De Meester, *Compendium Juris Canonici*, I, 174.

[57] A reply of S. C. de Religiosis, 3 Nov. 1923, (*A. A. S.*, XVI [1924], 95), while referring directly only to the prescriptions of canon 505, furnishes the basis for the conclusion that the ones in charge of these houses are not really superiors.

[58] Vito, *Il Sinodo Diocesano*, p. 32, note 1.

[59] Cc. 495-497.

the bishop grants that permission. In case the provincial has his ordinary residence in the diocese,[60] he is permitted but not obliged to assist personally at the synod as the representative of his institute. If he does exercise this right, no other superior may attend.

Article II. Invited Members

The second paragraph of canon 358 gives the bishop the power to call others to the synod besides the ones who have a strict right to be present. The only condition necessary that the bishop may exercise this faculty is expressed in the words: ". . . si opportunum iudicaverit . . ." There are many circumstances which may prompt a bishop to invite more of the clergy than the strictly required number. It will be particularly prudent to do so in the event that the bishop wishes the synod to treat of the reformation of the clergy or of something that concerns them particularly, or when the decrees of the provincial council are to be promulgated or explained.[61] Even when there are not such important reasons, a bishop will always do well to invite to the synod as many of the clergy as can be spared for that short time from the pastoral work. Certainly the very notion of the synod itself and the history of the legislation concerning it should incline a bishop to regard this step not only as a right that he may exercise but as apt to bring to the diocese the marked benefits the Church intends it should.

The ones whom the Code explicitly states may be called to the synod are the rest of the clergy who in the first paragraph are given the right only to be represented. The bishop is permitted, but cannot be obliged, to invite all the canons of the collegiate churches, all the pastors and parochial vicars with full parochial powers, and all the local superiors of the religious institutes of the diocese.[62] He may even invite all the diocesan priests no matter what their work

[60] Toso, *Commentaria Minora,* III, 191.

[61] Blat, *Commentarium Codicis,* II, 329-330.

[62] The Code states in general terms *"Superiores religiosos."* Ayrinhac (*Constitution of the Church,* p. 199), Blat (*Commentarium Codicis,* II, 329) and Cocchi (*Commentarium in Codicem,* II, 237) interpret these words as referring only to the superiors of clerical religious. Vito (*Il Sinodo Diocesano,* p. 35) declares, however, that the superiors of lay institutes of the diocese are also included. Because of the connection between the first and second paragraph, ap-

may be, or at least as many as are not necessary for the spiritual needs of the faithful. In his invitation the bishop should state explicitly that the invited members are being called to the synod not because of a right to be present but because he deems their assistance advisable. It is even well to mention in the invitation the principal reasons for their presence.[63] Besides, as the Code states, the invited members have the same right to vote upon all matters as those who have a strict right to be called, unless the bishop makes it clear in his invitation that they are to assist without the right to vote. As a consequence the bishop should state explicitly in the invitation whether or not they are to have an active voice in the proceedings.

The question naturally arises concerning the power of the bishop to invite others than those explicitly mentioned in the canon. From the text of the law and its apparent contextual connection with the first paragraph it does not seem as if the bishop is given the positive right to convoke others if he wishes. The words: "*. . . et etiam . . . imo et . . .*" apparently indicate the limit of the bishop's power of convocation.[64] In other words, the sense of the entire canon seems to be that there are some the bishop is obliged to convoke and there are others whom he can convoke. Who they are in both cases is stated explicitly. With these provisions the legislator has given the bishop the means by which he is able to hold the synod with the best possible results. All who have an interest in the proceedings can be present or at least have a representative there. There will hardly ever be need to summon anyone else. However, in case a bishop would find it advisable to have one not mentioned in the second paragraph, as for example an extra-diocesan priest, a religious, or even a lay person [65] present at the synod in order to obtain their

parently the first opinion is to be preferred. Although the expression is unqualified, for the same reason it includes only the minor local superiors.

[63] Vito, *Il Sinodo Diocesano*, p. 36.

[64] Ayrinhac, *Constitution of the Church*, p. 199; Vito, *Il Sinodo Diocesano*, p. 35.

[65] Benedict XIV (*De Synodo Dioecesana*, 1. III, c. 9, n. 8) admitted that a bishop could invite the laity to the synod whenever there was a legitimate custom or a grave reason for their presence but excluded them from taking active part in the proceedings.

counsel about certain matters, there is nothing to prevent him from doing so. Although he has not the right by law to convoke such persons, he is not forbidden to do so. Apparently the difference would be in the fact that such persons could not be obliged to accept the invitation. At the same time it would seem that if they came the bishop would have no power to give them the right to vote in any of the proceedings.

A second question that arises is whether the faculty of the bishop to invite those mentioned in the second paragraph of this canon can be changed into an obligation to invite them. The fact, it might be urged, that a bishop has always invited certain priests to the synod could very well become a legitimate custom obliging later bishops of the diocese to call them to the synod. Would this then, if certainly established, deprive a bishop of the right given by the Code to convoke these priests or not as he sees fit? Vito [66] holds that such a custom must be regarded as contrary to the Code, and therefore subject to the norms of canon 5. The legislator in an attempt to accommodate the requirements of the synod to present conditions and to stabilize the synod as an integral part of Church government, has changed considerably the previous legislation in regard to the membership of the synod. The bishop has been given broad powers in this matter to use as he sees fit. Therefore, it would nullify the advantages of such changes if legal custom were able to deprive a bishop of the rights given him. For this reason, therefore, any custom obliging a bishop to invite others than those mentioned in the first paragraph must be regarded as null and void. In case there is a centenary or immemorial custom, it can be tolerated by the bishop if he deems it inadvisable to remove it. However, he alone is the judge and should disregard the custom as soon as circumstances permit. For the same reason, any prescription of particular law, as for example that of the Second Plenary Council of Baltimore [67] commanding that "omnes etiam in dignitatibus quibuscumque constituti" should be called to the synod, is no longer binding. It has become contrary to the law of the Code and consequently according to canon 6 1° has lost its legal value.

[66] *Il Sinodo Diocesano*, pp. 37-38.

[67] *Acta et Decreta*, n. 66.

ARTICLE III. OBLIGATION OF ATTENDANCE

The prescriptions of the Code granting some of the clergy the right to be present at the synod and the bishop the power to convoke others would be useless unless there was also imposed on at least some of these the obligation to attend. Otherwise it might be impossible to hold the synod because a proper membership could not be obtained.

1. *The Obligated Members*

It is certain that the clergy listed in canon 358 §1 have not only the right to be called to the synod but are obliged to attend. The words: "... *ad eamque venire debent* ..." leave no doubt as to the existence of this obligation. Of course it is implied that they are not to depart from the synod until it is completed. Only when they have been legitimately excused according to canon 359 §1 does the obligation of attendance cease. The legislator in limiting the number of the clergy who must be called to the synod has prescribed that only the ones whose presence is especially desirable have to be summoned. This minimum is necessary if the idea of a synod as a diocesan consultative body is not to be lost. Vito [68] even insists that if any of those mentioned in the first paragraph are absent from the synod without being legitimately excused the synod as such is invalid. Moreover, although the legislation has force, it is not synodal. The reason he gives is that they can be forced by canonical penalties to come. However, the invalidity is neither expressly nor equivalently stated in the law, and therefore according to canon 11 cannot be urged.

There is a controversy among authors as to whether the clergy whom the second paragraph permits the bishop to call to the synod are obliged to come if they are invited. By far the majority of present day authors [69] believe that only the ones mentioned in the first

[68] *Il Sinodo Diocesano*, p. 23, note 1.

[69] Ferrerres, *Institutiones Canonicae*, I, 253; De Meester, *Juris Canonici Compendium*, II, 174; Wernz-Vidal, *De Personis*, p. 669; Augustine, *Rights and Duties of Ordinaries*, p. 96; Toso, *Commentaria Minora*, III, 191; Muniz, *Procedimentos Ecclesiasticos*, I, 495; Coronata, *Institutiones Juris Canonici*, I, 477, note 3; Vromant, *Jus Missionariorum*, II, 178; Oesterle, *Praelectiones Juris Canonici*, I, 183.

paragraph are bound to attend. They insist that any others of the clergy whom the bishop may call are not obliged to be present because they are referred to in the canon as *invitati;* as Augustine argues, "they are merely invited and hence are free to come or not to come and the bishop cannot inflict any penalty for non-attendance." Apparently these authors place too much stress on the word *invitati* and do not take into account that in the first part of the same paragraph *vocare* is used, which admittedly has a stronger significance. Hence because some are spoken of as invited, it does not prove that the legislator does not intend to oblige them to come.

It seems therefore, as the other authors [70] maintain, that whenever any of the clergy are invited by the bishop they have the duty to assist at the synod. It is true that the legislator does not explicitly state that there is an obligation to attend as was done in the case of those listed in the first paragraph. However since the right of obligated members to attend the synod was clearly indicated, it was necessary to set forth their obligation in equally certain terms so as to prevent the possibility of their believing that this was a right to be exercised or not as they willed: "Ad synodum vocandi sunt ad eamque venire debent . . ." In the second paragraph of the canon, however, the legislator allows the bishop to invite the other clergy of the diocese to the synod. Nothing is said about a right on their part to attend. Consequently it was unnecessary to declare explicitly that they would be obliged to assist. Certainly it was clearly implied in the power given to the bishop; for otherwise his right would be useless.

The norm for determining in practice the obligation of invited members to attend the synod is the principal of canon 6 4°, which ordains that if it is not certain that the new law differs from the old law the latter must be followed. Accordingly invited members will be obliged to attend the synod if their presence was prescribed by the Tridentine law. All priests in the diocese who are engaged in the ministry, whether they are pastors or not, and the local superiors of clerical institutes which do not have a general chapter, will

[70] Chelodi, *Jus de Personis,* p. 399; Pistocchi, *De Synodo Dioecesana,* p. 39; Ayrinhac, *Constitution of the Church,* p. 200. Probably because of the use of the word *convocare* Vermeersch also maintains this opinion.—Cf. *Epitome,* I, 252.

be obliged to assist at the synod if they are invited by the bishop. The remaining clergy referred to in the second paragraph have not a similar obligation by reason of this canon.

2. *Legitimate Absence*

Of course, it may happen that the clergy who are obliged to be present at the synod will find it physically or morally impossible to attend. The legislator, accordingly, has implied in canon 359 §1 that a legitimate excuse for absence must be considered, as for example a serious illness. However, because it is obligatory to have only a representation of the clergy at the synod, one could not be excused because of his pastoral duties; for a substitute vicar could be appointed from the clergy not attending the synod. In general, the excuse must be proportionate to the obligation and will vary with particular circumstances.

However, it is not the one prevented from attending who will decide whether or not the excuse is sufficient. Canon 359 §1 implies that the decision rests with the bishop. Thus, he must always be informed. If it is at all possible, the notification should be made before the synod is celebrated so that the bishop will have an opportunity to judge whether the excuse is sufficient and to call another if he wishes. In the event that this is impossible, an explanation of one's absence should be given as soon as it is convenient. In addition it is also necessary to receive permission of the bishop to leave the synod before it is concluded. If either the excuse to absent oneself or to depart before the end of the synod is not satisfactory to the bishop and nevertheless one remains contumacious after being informed, he may be punished according to the norms of the second paragraph.[71]

It is stated in this canon, moreover, that the clergy legitimately excused have not any right to send a proxy in their place. Although this concession is made to any who are legitimately prevented from attending the ecumenical, plenary or provincial council,[72] it is not allowed in the case of absentees from the synod because the circumstances are different. First of all, the requirements for the synod

[71] Wernz-Vidal, *De Personis*, p. 670.

[72] Cc. 234 §1, 287 §1.

have been so changed that the need of a proxy will seldom arise. Then, the clergy who are obliged to come are only those who because of their office are presumed to have a special competence on the matters to be treated. The principal reason, however, is that at the councils there is a question of a deliberative vote of which one should not be deprived; while at the synod in practically all the matters only the bishop determines what is to be adopted. However, it is to be noted that the right of sending a proxy is denied only to the members. Therefore, the bishop is not forbidden to designate one to act in this capacity, even if that be one whom otherwise he could not invite. In such a case the one chosen would not be acting in his own name.

3. *Punishment of Absentees*

In order to insure the observance of the obligation to attend the synod when the bishop convokes it, the Code explicitly grants him the right to compel any who should be present to attend the synod or to punish them afterwards with suitable penalties if they are absent without due reason. The bishop is allowed to punish all those listed in canon 358 §1 as well as the clergy invited to the synod who were bound by the Tridentine law to attend the synod, that is, all who are in the care of souls and the religious superiors who are not subject to a general chapter. The only exception to this regulation is explicitly stated in canon 359 §2, according to which exempt religious cannot be punished for non-attendance unless they are pastors; and, apparently, although the word *parochi* is used, this includes, besides the religious who in extraordinary cases are permitted by the Apostolic Delegate to be pastors,[73] all the parochial vicars who have full parochial powers.[74] This restriction, as Pistocchi[75] and Vito[76] observe, is evidently a derogation from the principle enunciated in canon 619 according to which the Ordinary of the place has power to punish religious concerning all matters in which they are subject to him.

[73] Cf. Index Facultatum Legatorum Apostolicorum, n. 48—Vermeersch-Creusen, *Epitome,* I, 484.

[74] C. 451 §2 2°.

[75] *De Synodo Dioecesana,* p. 43.

[76] *Il Sinodo Diocesano,* p. 41.

CHAPTER VI

PREPARATION OF THE SYNOD

Canon 360. § 1. Episcopus, si id ipsi expedire videatur, opportuno ante Synodum tempore, unam vel plures e clero civitatis et dioecesis commissiones nominet, seu coetus virorum qui res in Synodo tractandas parent.

§ 2. Ante Synodi sessiones Episcopus omnibus qui convocati sunt et convenerunt, decretorum schema tradendum curet.

Canon 361. Propositae quaestiones omnes, praesidente vel per se vel per alium Episcopo, liberae adstantium disceptationi in sessionibus praeparatoriis subiiciantur.

In the Code the legislator has for the first time taken cognizance of the need of making certain preparations before the synod. The reason for the present prescriptions and recommendations is clear.

"From the very nature of the synod, as outlined in previous chapters, it follows that a definite and detailed preparation must be made if it is to be celebrated according to the letter and spirit of Canon Law and the ritual of the Church. It is an event which requires much deliberation on the part of the bishop, as well as diligence, study and patient arrangement of details on the part of those associated with him in this task. As in every work, but especially one of this kind, the greater and more painstaking the preparation the greater will be the success achieved and the more enduring the benefits derived. It is not too much to say that, if the synod is badly prepared, that is, in a careless and superficial manner, it will mean little more to a diocese than a mere formality complying with the letter of the law but not fulfilling its spirit, and consequently not producing the salutary fruits for the common welfare of both clergy and faithful which should be the result of such an assembly. The minutest details must be thoughtfully foreseen and provided for;

the statutes must be carefully drawn up by expert and prudent canonists. Everything should be so arranged that the greatest possible good may accrue to the diocese from the celebration of the synod." [1]

Article I. Pre-Synodal Commissions

1. *Appointment*

The first step to be taken by the bishop in preparing for the synod is to name certain commissions to draw up the synodal legislation. Because of its obvious advantages, even pre-Code authors suggested a similar preparation,[2] or at least advised that if commissions were not appointed the bishop should hold some preparatory meetings with a few advisers to decide on the laws to be enacted.[3] In canon 360 §1 it is now recommended that the bishop name one or more commissions to make a draft of the matters to be treated in the synod. Authors [4] agree, however, that because of the words ". . . *si id ipsi expedire videatur* . . ." the canon does not impose an obligation to appoint pre-synodal commissions but leaves their appointment to the discretion of the bishop. The provision is made because the bishop alone has the authority in the synod; and he therefore can arrange, as he sees fit, the matters which are to be discussed and adopted. In order to have the synod accomplish the most possible good for the diocese, a bishop will almost always find it advantageous to follow this recommendation of the Code. For the needs of the diocese will then be better known, and a collective study will undoubtedly make the remedies apt to be more effective. It is necessary, of course, for the bishop to name these commissions sufficiently before the synod to give the members ample time to draw up correct and well-defined statutes. It might be suggested that the names of the members and the place where they are to meet be in-

[1] McGuigan, *Diocesan Synod,* Part III, 73-74.

[2] Benedict XIV, *De Synodo Dioecesana,* l. II, c. 11, n. 3; l. XIII, c. 2, n. 7; Bouix, *De Episcopo,* II, 379-380; Phillips, *Compendium Juris Ecclesiastici,* p. 377; Wernz, *Jus Decretalium,* II b, 739.

[3] Cappello, *De Visitatione Liminum,* I, 314-315.

[4] Blat, *Commentarium Codicis,* II, 331; Wernz-Vidal, *De Personis,* p. 673; Toso, *Commentaria Minora,* III, 192; Magnin, *Le Canoniste Contemporain,* XLVI (1924), 266; Vito, *Il Sinodo Diocesano,* p. 43.

cluded in the decree of their appointment, so that the rest of the clergy may be able to communicate their opinions and suggestions.

The number of the commissions must, as the Code implies, be determined by the needs of the diocese and the number of available priests who are capable of doing this work. Perhaps the best arrangement for a diocese of the ordinary size is the appointment of five commissions. First of all, it will be well to have a general commission to supervise and coordinate the work of the other commissions. The other four commisions can be arranged according to the order of the Code. One may prepare statutes on ecclesiastical persons, that is, concerning the clergy, religious and laity. The work of another may be statutes on the sacraments. Another may treat of sacred places and times, divine worship, and the teaching office of the Church. The final commission may concern itself with the remaining matters of ecclesiastical benefices and property. Such a division is, of course, arbitrary. But whatever arrangement is decided upon, it should adhere to the order of the Code, which then can serve as a guide to the commissions.

The Code makes no regulation about the membership of the commissions except in the statement that they be composed of clergy both of the city in which the synod is held and of the rest of the diocese. It does not seem, however, that the legislator intends to place a restriction on the bishop so that he could not invite extra-diocesan priests who are proficient in canon law to serve on the commissions.[5] For there is no reason why such assistance should be denied. It is preferable, though, that since the synod is concerned only with the diocese the bishop should as far as possible allow the diocesan priests to make the necessary arrangements. Only when they are not sufficiently competent should someone else be summoned. Because of the silence of the Code the bishop is perfectly free to choose the members of the commissions as he wishes and is under no obligation to include some of the cathedral chapter or board of consultors in their membership. However a very good arrangement is to appoint as chairman of each of the commissions, except for the general commission, one of the canons or consultors, and allow the others to serve as vice-chairmen. The vicar general may be placed in charge

[5] Cf. Magnin, *Le Canoniste Contemporain*, XLVI (1924), 266.

of the general commission. Besides these the vicars forane should be placed on the various commissions, since they are well acquainted with the conditions of the diocese.[6] The other members of the commissions can be drawn from both the diocesan and religious clergy and should include not only those whose prudence and keen insight into affairs and conditions in the diocese is recognized, but also the ones who are well versed in canonical matters. In this way the necessary reforms in ecclesiastical discipline will be made possible by wise canonical measures.

2. *Work of the Commissions*

In the first meeting of the pre-synodal commissions, at which the bishop should be present to give certain directions, it will probably be found more practical to divide the work of each commission among several groups or sub-committees of its members,[7] the number of which will depend on the extent of the commission's work. Thus a more concentrated preparation will be made possible. In their proposals besides drawing their recommendations from their own experience and that of their associates, the members of the sub-committees should take into consideration particularly the conditions which the bishop found at the time of his pastoral visitation.[8] Another most important source of the proposals should be the suggestions of the clergy of the diocese. Apparently too much emphasis cannot be laid on the fact that the success of the synod in a great measure depends on the freedom which the clergy are given in proffering their recommendations. Such freedom is important not only because of the distinct advantage it is to take into account everyone's point of view, but more so because the clergy must feel that their personal participation is of the very nature of the synod. It would therefore be preferable that, when appointing the commissions, the bishop announce that the clergy are perfectly free, if not to attend the meetings of the commissions, at least to send in their suggestions to the chairmen to be given proper consideration. Whenever all the sub-

[6] Cf. Veggian, *Il Sinodo Diocesano*, p. 28.

[7] D'Angelo, *La Curia Diocesana*, II, 215.

[8] Veggian, *Il Sinodo Diocesano*, p. 28; D'Angelo, *La Curia Diocesana*, II, 214.

committees have completed their tasks and a schema of proposals has been drawn up, they should be called together by their respective chairmen to submit their reports to the assembled commission.[9] After a complete examination and discussion, a draft of all the recommendations should be prepared and given to the general commission, which by itself or together with the other commissions should coordinate the proposals and submit them to the bishop, adding if they wish any further observations.

Once the bishop has given his original recommendations, it is usually better if he does not engage in the preparatory work of the commissions but leaves everything in their hands. Then, when they have completed their work and submitted the proposals, he may make a careful examination of all and approve, reject or decide the matters as he sees fit before the final schema is drafted.[10] The Code wisely has not given any set rule about procedure; that will have to vary according to conditions. But, whatever method is followed, there can be no doubt that the bishop has the final word about what will be included in the statutes after he has given due consideration to the recommendations of the commissions.

Article II. Appointment of Synodal Officials

There is no mention in the Code of the need of appointing officers for the synod. But, since the *Caeremoniale Episcoporum* [11] in its directions on the preparation of the synod indicates that a certain number are to be designated, the bishop ought to make the appointments in order to hold the synod properly.[12] While the Ceremonial

[9] Each commission may select one of its number to act as secretary to prepare a draft of its proposals. Cf. Vito, *Il Sinodo Diocesano,* p. 47, note 1.

[10] The secretary of the synod may be called upon to prepare the draft. It should be written in a clear, concise manner. Each regulation is usually formulated not as a canon but as a statute. (Cf. Benedict XIV, *De Synodo Dioecesana,* 1. I, c. 3, n. 2, 5; 1. VI, c. 2.) The statutes are usually written in Latin; but it is certainly permissible that they be in the vernacular if the bishop wishes them to be spread among the laity (Cf. D'Angelo, *La Curia Diocesana,* II, 215).

[11] L. I, c. 31, n. 18.

[12] Vito, *Il Sinodo Diocesano,* pp. 46-47. The synodal officials should be named soon after the synod is announced in order to allow each one sufficient time to make the necessary preparations. In selecting the officials the bishop

names especially notaries, porters, and masters of ceremonies, it is clear that there is no intention to prescribe any definite number. Circumstances in each place will determine the officials that are needed.[13] The following, however, may be indicated as necessary in every synod.

Promotor of the Synod. Usually it will be well to appoint the vicar general to this office. Briefly his duty as the representative of the bishop is to urge and insist upon the necessary arrangements, in order that the synod may be held according to the requirements of the Code and the wishes of the bishop. He must, first of all, make certain that all the preparations which the other officials are to make are being carefully carried out and that the pre-synodal commissions are doing their work properly and completing it in sufficient time for the synod. As regards his particular duties, he will arrange the seating according to the rules of precedence, have the schema of the proposed statutes distributed to the clergy, prepare for the preparatory sessions, direct the making of the profession of faith, have the statutes read in the synod if they are to be promulgated there, and finally arrange the approbation of the diocesan officials to be selected in the synod. If necessary, an assistant promotor may be appointed to give the required attention to these duties.

Secretary. Benedict XIV suggests that one of the chapter be appointed as secretary. Before the celebration of the synod he should formulate the various decrees that have to be published as well as prepare the final copy of the proposed statutes. His principal duty during the synod will be to take down an account of the various happenings in the preparatory and solemn sessions. He should list the names of the members of each session and with the assistance of several tellers tabulate the voting. Besides, at the beginning of the preparatory sessions the secretary will distribute copies of the proposed statutes and later collect them if the clergy have noted their

need not seek the advice of his chapter or consultors. Cf. Bouix, *De Episcopo*, II, 360.

[13] Cf. Benedict XIV, *De Synodo Dioecesana*, 1. IV, c. 1; Bargilliat, *Praelectiones Juris Canonici*, I, 463-464; D'Angelo, *La Curia Diocesana*, II, 216-217; Veggian, *Il Sinodo Diocesano*, pp. 34-37; *Praxis Synodalis*, pp. 24-29.

opinions and suggestions. The secretary proposes to the promotor of the synod the matters to be treated and publishes the various decrees at the order of the one who presides. Finally, if the statutes are to be promulgated in the synod, the secretary will read at least the principal statutes.

NOTARY. The chancellor of the curia may be appointed notary of the synod. Apart from the general duty of assisting the secretary particularly in taking the attendance and counting the votes, the notary should prepare a brief account of the synod from the principal events recorded by the secretary. The summarized report can be published with the statutes.

MASTER OF CEREMONIES. In order to make sure that the synod is celebrated according to the regulations of the Ceremonial and the Pontifical, the bishop should designate at least one master of ceremonies. In addition to attending beforehand to the proper arrangement and decoration of the church, the master of ceremonies must at the opening of the synod arrange that the procession and seating of the clergy is according to the rules of precedence. Throughout the synod, with the aid of those whom he has chosen, he must attend to the exact and prompt observance of what is set down in the liturgical books.

PROCURATOR OF THE CLERGY. Although canon 361 prescribes a free discussion by the clergy of the proposed statutes, it is not implied that a procurator cannot be chosen to whom the clergy may submit their opinions and suggestions, either orally or in writing. Indeed the appointment of a procurator is to be recommended in order to allow any of the clergy who do not wish to proffer their recommendations personally to submit their opinions to the procurator. However, the bishop cannot command the clergy to do this, since the Code allows the freedom of discussion. Moreover as the spokesman for the clergy, the procurator should endeavor to have the bishop modify any statutes which are not favorably regarded.

With regard to other officials mentioned by the authors—judge of excuses for absence, prefects for the balloting, prefects of discipline, confessors, preachers, and porters—for the proper celebration of the synod there is no need that they be appointed. However, the bishop may do as he sees fit.

Article III. Preparatory Sessions

As Gousset, a former Archbishop of Rheims,[14] points out, a free discussion by the clergy of the laws which the bishop intends to adopt is of the essence of the synod. If the synod is to consist merely in a reading of statutes definitely decided upon by the bishop without any prior discussion or explanation, the holding of the synod is unnecessary. It would be equally as good to publish the decrees in some other way as purely episcopal laws. Consequently the Code in canon 361 obliges the bishop to hold the preparatory sessions, the number of which are to be determined by the matters to be discussed. The words ". . . *in sessionibus praeparatoriis subiiciantur*" must be interpreted in this sense.[15] The opinion of Augustine [16] that the Code only suggests but does not command these sessions cannot be sustained. This prescription is expressed differently from that concerning the appointment of pre-synodal commissions which the bishop is to name ". . . *si id ipsi expedire videatur.*" Perhaps the opinion of Magnin,[17] who maintains that the preparatory sessions would not be necessary if the discussion was assured in some other way, likewise cannot be accepted; for the Code does not imply that an alternative suffices. There is nothing in the Code to indicate at what time the preparatory sessions are to be held. Commentators [18] seem to imply that the preparatory meetings should take place simultaneously with the solemn sessions. This arrangement will not permit sufficient time for proper consideration of the arguments and suggestions of

[14] *Exposition des Principes du Droit Canonique*, pp. 323-324.

[15] Chelodi, *Jus de Personis*, p. 397, note 4; Coronata, *Institutiones Juris Canonici*, I, 479, note 1.

[16] *Rights and Duties of Ordinaries*, p. 96.

[17] *Le Canoniste Contemporain*, XLVI (1924), 267.

[18] Chelodi, *Jus de Personis*, p. 400; Vermeersch-Creusen, *Epitome*, I, 252; De Meester, *Compendium Juris Canonici*, I, 177; Vito, *Il Sinodo Diocesano*, pp. 49-51.

the clergy, in the event that the final draft of the states is to be promulgated in the synod. Therefore it might be suggested that, if it is at all feasible, the preparatory sessions be held prior to the synod. Thus the secretary will have ample time to put the statutes in their final form after the recommendations of the clergy have been carefully examined by the bishop.

There are no details given in the Code about the preparatory sessions. Since under the present law these meetings are an integral part of the synod,[19] the same regulations must be followed as for the regular solemn sessions.[20] Accordingly the membership of the preparatory sessions will be the same and absence must be judged as absence from any of the solemn sessions. Moreover, the same order of precedence is to be followed. There is not, however, any necessity to make the profession of faith in these sessions, as Pistocchi [21] maintains, since the Code in canon 1406 §1 1° does not prescribe that it be made in the beginning of the synod. The profession should be postponed until the first solemn session of the synod, as the Pontifical arranges. It is the bishop, as canon 361 states, who has the right to preside over the preparatory sessions. He may delegate another to preside in his place. In fact it will usually be advisable to have someone else preside in order to insure as frank a discussion as possible. The promotor of the synod will be most suitable for the office.

Before the preparatory sessions are opened, a schema of the proposed statutes should be given to the clergy. Authors [22] agree that canon 360 §2 imposes this obligation on the bishop in order that the clergy may know the content of the proposed legislation before the synod begins. Moreover the schema, according to the text of the law, is to be given to all who have been convoked and have come. Pistoc-

[19] Vito, *Il Sinodo Diocesano*, p. 49.

[20] It would not be necessary, however, to hold the preparatory sessions in the church. Any large hall may be used which is a suitable place for the discussion. Cf. Vito, *o. c.*, p. 51.

[21] *De Synodo Dioecesana*, p. 47.

[22] Chelodi, *Jus de Personis*, p. 400; Coronata, *Institutiones Juris Canonici*, I, 478; Vito, *Il Sinodo Diocesano*, p. 46; Toso, *Commentaria Minora*, III, 192; Wernz-Vidal, *De Personis*, p. 673. However, Augustine (*Rights and Duties of Ordinaries*, p. 96) does not regard this as an obligation.

chi [23] and Vito [24] accordingly point out that it may not be sent to the clergy before they have arrived for the synod. Magnin [25] does not consider that the freedom of the bishop is thus limited but maintains that a minimum is stated, that is, that the members of the synod should know of the decrees at least before the synod begins. He implies that a schema may be sent to the clergy previous to the preparatory sessions so as to give them ample time to examine it. Although this view appears preferable in practice, it seems to be against the text of the law. Therefore the interpretation of the other authors must be retained.

The discussion in the preparatory sessions must be entirely free. The only limitation that ought to be imposed is that the debate be moderated by the one presiding. Everyone who has come to the synod with the right to vote should be permitted to express his suggestions. Even if there is a procurator for the clergy, no member should be denied the right to proffer his opinion personally. This freedom is necessary if the synod is to bring to the diocese the benefits which the Church expects it to produce. When the discussion has ended, it will be well to have a balloting of ratification in writing, in which what is not acceptable may be indicated. Though this vote can only be consultative, the bishop will then know exactly the opinion of his clergy and can make the final decision with that in mind.

[23] *De Synodo Dioecesana,* p. 46.

[24] *Il Sinodo Diocesano,* p. 46.

[25] *Le Canoniste Contemporain,* XLVI (1924), 267.

CHAPTER VII

SYNODAL LEGISLATION

THE principal work of the synod is the legislation which is to be enacted there. It was in good part the recognized need of a diocesan legislative body that gave rise to the synod and which ever since has prompted the Church to endeavor to stabilize it as an integral part of ecclesiastical government. Although in the course of time other matters have come under its competence, the primary purpose of the synod has continued to be the consideration and adoption of local laws. It is important, however, in order that these ordinances have legal force, that they be confined to the sphere assigned by the superior legislator. A chapter on the synodal legislation is presented to indicate the general principles that must be observed in formulating synodal statutes. No attempt will be made to give an exhaustive list of possible particular legislation. The purpose of this chapter is to point out the norms which have been laid down in the common law for particular legislation. This will be done in the following two articles. The first will treat of the object of the synodal statutes in general, and the second of special types of law which at times it may be necessary to incorporate in the statutes.

ARTICLE I. OBJECT OF THE SYNODAL STATUTES

Since there is in the Code an orderly and complete arrangement of the present general law of the Church, the formulation of synodal legislation becomes easier. For the statutes may very well be compiled as supplementary to the Code. Thus, on the one hand, the Code will be a collection of general laws made necessary by the circumstances to be found usually throughout the Church. The synodal statutes, on the other hand, will provide regulations demanded by the peculiar conditions of each diocese which the common law cannot take into account. It will be the purpose of the statutes to provide more specific legislation than the general prescriptions of the

Code. Therefore, because of this similarity between the two, the statutes should not treat of doctrinal matters. Their object should be entirely disciplinary.[1] Likewise it is advisable that the order of the statutes be the same as that of the Code to facilitate their joint use. In this way the statutes are likely to be more effective.

1. *Extent of the Synodal Statutes*

Briefly the extent of the statutes is whatever concerns the spiritual welfare of the diocese and has not already been sufficiently provided for in higher law. The words of canon 356 §1 ". . . in qua de iis tantum agendum quae ad particulares cleri populique dioecesis necessitates vel utilitates referuntur" express very clearly the competence of the synod. Within its proper limits it can adopt whatever measures are deemed by the bishop, after the required consultation with members of the synod, not only necessary but even useful for the welfare of either the clergy or laity of the diocese. And in both instances the regulations enacted, as true law, oblige in conscience the ones for whom they are made. More particularly the competence of the synod may be divided as follows: (1) it can urge that the law of the Code be better observed; (2) it can determine more definitely matters treated only substantially by the Code; (3) it can make provisions on matters not mentioned in the Code. An earnest attempt to treat these points carefully in the synod will be of immeasurable benefit to the diocese.

The first legislative office of the synod is to insist on the exact observance of the common law. This is given in the words of canon 336 §1, "Observantiam legum ecclesiasticarum Episcopi urgeant . . .," as the first duty of the bishop. He must strive to prevent abuses from creeping into the entire ecclesiastical discipline, but be particularly vigilant in regard to the administration of the sacraments and sacramentals, divine worship, preservation of the faith, religious instruction for the young, preaching, indulgences, and the exact fulfillment of pious bequests. A bishop is obliged to this vigilance by reason of his pastoral office. The synod offers an excellent opportunity to attend to the obligation most effectively. For if the pre-

[1] Veggian, *Il Sinodo Diocesano*, p. 30.

synodal commissions function properly and the preparatory sessions are held with the intent of giving the clergy complete liberty in expressing their opinions, conditions should be seen exactly as they are and the remedies chosen should be more effective. However the mere repetition of canons of the Code in the synodal statutes is not the way in which to promote a better observance of the common law. A bishop may use the occasion of the synod to speak to the assembled clergy of the disregarded laws. But, since the statutes are intended to be supplementary to the Code, to contain what the Code has not provided for, it is preferable not to incorporate its canons in the statutes. In fact, if the canons of the Code are not heeded it is not likely that greater attention will be given them as statutes.

The only means to be taken to promote a better observance of the general law in the diocese by synodal statutes is, if urgently necessary, to enact penal sanctions. If the Code contains non-reserved penalties, the absolution or dispensation from these may be reserved, or additional sanctions may be imposed.[2] Adding penalties to a higher law is clearly not a derogation from the rights of the superior legislator. On the contrary it aids what he is trying to promote.[3] In this connection, however, it is important to remember the advice of the Council of Trent [4] which is repeated in canon 2214 §2 of the Code. Bishops are to be mindful that the exercise of their office is ever to be fatherly, and therefore that penalties should be imposed only when other means have failed and then in a spirit of kindness with the intention of helping the wrong-doers and deterring others from similar faults. That will mean that penalties will be imposed only with great circumspection. Accordingly, in addition to the fact that the delict to which the penal sanction is added must be an external act, grave either in itself or by reason of special circumstances,[5] there should also be some added gravity that demands the penalty.[6] The existence of grave consequences must be particularly verified if the penalty is to be a censure,[7] which in addition can pun-

[2] Cf. c. 2221; Sole, *De Delictis et Poenis,* p. 62.

[3] Reiffenstuel, *Jus Canonicum,* I, 119.

[4] Sess. XIII, *de reformatione,* c. 1.

[5] Cf. cc. 2195 §1, 2218 §1.

[6] Cf. Benedict XIV, *De Synodo Dioecesana,* l. X, c. 1, n. 3.

[7] C. 2241 §2.

ish only a consummated act.[8] Moreover, the penal law should be framed absolutely and not conditionally, and express clearly and exactly the kind of penalty that is imposed,[9] what it punishes, and those whom it binds.[10] In the event that there is a very peculiar gravity about the matter, the Code implies that the bishop may reserve to himself the absolution from censures, whether they are of common law or particular law.[11] But the reservation must be stated expressly in the statute.[12] The bishop cannot, however, add a reserved censure to a law which the Holy See has already punished by a censure reserved to itself.[13]

The synodal statutes should also include the necessary determinations of common law. The synod ought, first of all, examine the questions explicitly assigned by the Code to be decided upon preferably in the synod; namely, the determination of which is the nearer parish according to canon 472 2°, the settling of the diocesan stipend according to canon 831 §1, the reservation of sins according to canon 895, and the defining of a stipend that may be exacted under certain conditions prescribed in canon 1333 §2 and §4. Moreover, the Code insinuates statutory legislation concerning the faculties of vicars forane.[14] and the obligation of residence for assistants (*vicarii cooperatores*).[15] Finally, there are certain matters left by the Code to be determined by each bishop which may very well be settled in the synod and included in the statutes, as for example the details of the clerical examinations provided for in canon 130 §1; regulations concerning the celebration of mass by extra-diocesan priests according to canon 804 §3; the distance that will permit burial outside the

[8] C. 2242 §1. However, as c. 2228 implies, this does not mean an attempt at a crime could not be threatened with a censure. Cf. Vermeersch-Creusen, *Epitome*, III, 216; Dargin, *Reserved Cases*, p. 47.

[9] According to canon 2255 §2, excommunication must always be a censure; interdict and suspension may be either a censure or a vindicative penalty. When the time is determined, penalties are vindicative; and, when they are not, they are censures. Cf. Dargin, *Reserved Cases*, p. 45.

[10] Cf. Cappello, *De Censuris*, pp. 35-36.

[11] C. 2246 §1.

[12] C. 2245 §4.

[13] C. 2247 §1.

[14] C. 447.

[15] C. 476 §5.

parish church according to canon 1218 §2; and the offerings for funerals according to canon 1234 §1. In addition synodal laws may prescribe exactly how obligations imposed by the Code are to be carried out. Although the common law has imposed the substantial obligation, particular law may ordain the manner, the place, the time, or other circumstances under which the obligation is to be fulfilled. This would not be trespassing on the rights of the higher legislator. On the contrary, by accommodating the general law to local conditions, it insures a more exact observance of what he is endeavoring to stabilize.

The final and chief source of the matter of the synodal statutes is what may be termed as being *praeter legem.* Here are included the many points about which, because of the varying local conditions, the Code or even plenary and provincial decrees have made no provision and which, however, should be decided to enable priests in the ministry to do their work properly. Besides one must classify as *praeter legem* the questions concerning which there is a controversy among canonists whether or not provisions have been made in the law and which therefore because of canon 15 do not oblige in practice. The synod can legislate on these matters and establish a certain obligation for the diocese. As Benedict XIV [16] shows by many examples, no exhaustive list of points *praeter legem* could be given because of the diversity of conditions. Keen observance at the time of the episcopal visitation, prudent study by the members of the pre-synodal commissions, and the practical experience of the clergy, will make known the matters to be legislated on in the synod. Among many others a few that may be suggested are: erection of buildings, parish insurance, government and upkeep of cemeteries for more than one parish, support of orphanages and other charitable institutions, maintenance of diocesan high schools, catechetical instruction for students of elementary and secondary public schools, frequency of missions, ministrations to the sick, clerical conferences, retreats for priests, rules of clerical life, salary of the clergy, stole fees, rights of chaplains, procedure for the care of Orientals, communication with the chancery office, and regulations concerning information for the diocesan tribunal. Whatever is deemed

[16] *De Synodo Dioecesana,* l. VI, c. 3-11.

necessary or advisable may be prescribed and sanctioned by suitable penalties.

2. *Limitations of the Statutes*

Canon 335 §1 states that the legislative power of the bishop must be exercised according to the norms of the sacred canons. Consequently care must be taken that the synodal statutes conform to the limitations imposed in the common law. Thus laws should not be enacted on questions which are expressly removed from the competence of the bishop. Moreover, the synodal legislation ought not be opposed to existing higher laws. Finally, privileges and certain legal customs should be respected.

First of all the legislative power of the bishop, and therefore of the synod, cannot touch matters which are outside his competence. For many centuries, particularly up to the thirteenth, the extent of the legislative power of the bishop was very broad and, as a study of the evolution of much of the present canonical discipline shows, it is to episcopal regulations that very many present laws owe their origin. But during this period the sections of the Church were much more isolated than they are now, and there was relatively little influx from one part to another. Therefore differences in important points of discipline were not liable to cause much difficulty. Since then, however, this condition has changed. Improved means of travel have resulted in a large amount of constant moving not only from one section of a country to another, but even from one nation to another and one continent to another. If, therefore, certain important points of discipline were not withdrawn from the competence of individual bishops and reserved to the Holy See, even though it might be advantageous for a diocese that additions be made to the already existing general law, the result for so many would be a hopeless confusion. An example of what might be expected can be gathered from the practical difficulties which jurists here in the United States experience on important matters of civil law because one jurisdiction is not always obliged by what another has adopted. The Code has denied bishops the right to legislate on certain matters which, if permitted, might result in a similar confusion. Thus, only the Holy See can institute irregularities of sacred orders,[17] impeding

[17] C. 983. Cf. Hickey, *Irregularities and Simple Impediments*, pp. 12-13.

and diriment matrimonial impediments,[18] and feast days and days of fast and abstinence.[19] Likewise a bishop cannot legislate on matters that the Code has reserved to the provincial council or provincial gathering of bishops, as for example the determination of the cathedraticum and other taxes,[20] or even points which these gatherings have reserved to themselves. Therefore, before the statutes are enacted, an inquiry should be made as to whether any such restrictions exist which remove the matters from the competence of the synod.

Another limitation imposed upon the bishop is not to make laws which are opposed to prescriptions of higher law. Accordingly it is forbidden to enact legislation opposed to a command or a prohibition of higher law either because it attempts to repeal what is commanded, permit what is forbidden, or lastly impose an obligation repugnant to it.[21] Such prescriptions are clearly contrary to the law of the superior. It must be noted, however, that legislation of an inferior legislator is without legal force only if the higher law is certainly binding. If there is a doubt of law among canonists about the question, the bishop is not forbidden to make a contrary enactment. The reason is, of course, the principle stated in canon 15, that a doubtful law does not oblige in practice. An inferior legislator may consider it as non-existent and proceed according to that fact until an authentic interpretation has been given. While in theory opposition between laws would appear to be able to be easily perceived, in practice it is often difficult to determine whether or not a real opposition exists. Therefore both must be closely studied before the invalidity of the inferior law can be definitely stated.

Similarly a bishop cannot interfere with what the higher law has permitted by attempting to repeal or forbid the use of the permission or to impose an obligation incompatible with it. But the higher

[18] C. 1038 §2.

[19] C. 1244 §1, 2. The Ordinary of the place is permitted to announce feast days and days of fast and abstinence "per modum tantum actus," but he may not ordain that this regulation continue habitually or permanently. Cf. Coronata, *De Locis et Temporibus Sacris*, p. 278; Vermeersch-Creusen, *Epitome*, III, 322.

[20] Cc. 1504, 1507 §1, 1909 §1.

[21] Suarez, *De Legibus*, 1. VI, c. 27, n. 2.

law must actually give the permission. And consequently, because the law fails to prohibit some act, it does not follow that a legal permission has been established, for the reason, which Suarez points out,[22] that the legislator has not acted to manifest his will. It is only when there has been a positive declaration that the legal permission comes into existence or, as Suarez puts it: "ut ergo sit proprie permissus per legem, ***oportet ut ipsa permissio stabiliatur et firmetur aliquo decreto et voluntate legislatoris:*** et tunc recte dicitur actus permissus positive, et similiter permissio illa habet specialem modum, ratione cujus dicatur effectus legis." Accordingly a law which only doubtfully grants a permission cannot be considered to forbid an opposing law of an inferior legislator. The permission must be expressly and certainly stated in the law.[23] The law grants a legal permission either by positively conceding a right and legal capacity to perform a certain act,[24] or by allowing the performance of an act which is not essentially evil, or finally by granting legal impunity to an act which is intrinsically wrong.[25] In all of these cases a true legal right is given.[26] A permission of law, of course, imposes no obligation on the one to whom it is granted. It is a right to be used or not. The obligation that arises is imposed on others not to prevent the use of the right. Thus it is that the bishop as the legislator of the synod cannot violate any legal permission even when he attempts to eradicate abuses of the right. The limit of his power is, as Benedict XIV [27] points out, to demand that before the right be exercised he view the case so as to determine whether or not the conditions implicitly intended by higher law are actually present. In this way abuses can be eliminated. In practice, however, the violation of

[22] *De Legibus*, 1. I, c. 15, n. 8.

[23] Wernz, *Jus Decretalium*, II b, 543; *A. A. S.*, XIII (1921), 228.

[24] Cf. c. 838, which allows priests to send Mass stipends to any others who are evidently in good standing or recommended by their own Ordinary. S. Cong. of the Council on February 19, 1921, decided that a provincial decree that restricted this right could not be sustained—*A. A. S.*, XIII (1921), 228-230.

[25] Cf. e. g. c. 855 §2 according to which in the absence of scandal occult sinners should not be denied the reception of Holy Communion.

[26] Cf. Maroto, *Institutiones Juris Canonici*, I, 228-229; Michiels, *Normae Generales*, I, 254-256; Van Hove, *De Legibus Ecclesiasticis*, p. 162.

[27] *De Synodo Dioecesana*, 1. III, c. 5, n. 9.

permissive laws is hard to determine; and therefore this question will often offer many serious difficulties.

The final limitations placed on the legislative power of the bishop are rights given by certain privileges and legal customs. With regard to the former all that need be said is that the bishop has no power to legislate contrary to what special privileges grant, either by revoking them directly or indirectly through an opposing law, except when he or his predecessor has granted them. As regards customs which are established according to legitimate norms he cannot legislate in opposition to these, either by directly revoking them or by making a law incompatible with the observance of the custom, whenever they have been established by the consent of a superior legislator. The reason is that the customs have become similar to the laws of the superior.[28] In any other instance opposing laws are unquestionably valid.

Article II. Special Types of Synodal Laws

Oftentimes conditions in a diocese will demand a special type of law in order to insure the proper ecclesiastical discipline. Therefore, it may be well to indicate in a general way the norms which must be observed that these laws may have legal force. Accordingly invalidating or inhabilitating laws, personal laws, laws for *peregrini,* and laws for Orientals will be discussed.

1. *Invalidating and Inhabilitating Laws*

There were some pre-Code authors who denied the power of the bishop to make invalidating and inhabilitating laws. Wernz[29] maintained that this power existed since there was no prohibition of it expressed in the law. Certainly there is not a general prohibition contained in the Code, apart from the particular instance of not establishing diriment impediments to matrimony. In the absence of restriction, therefore, invalidating and inhabilitating laws may be included in the synodal statutes as often as they are deemed necessary.

[28] Cf. Michiels, *Normae Generales,* II, 37-39, 122-124.

[29] *Jus Decretalium,* I, 111-112.

However the prescription of canon 11 must be observed. That is, the nullity of the act or the inhability of the person must be stated in the law either expressly or equivalently. Since authors disagree on the phrases that are to be comprehended under these generic terms,[30] it is advisable in practice to state explicitly that the act is null or the person is incapable, as the case may be. Thus many difficulties of interpretation will be prevented.

2. *Personal Laws*

Previous to the Code some authors denied that the bishop had power to make personal laws, that is, laws which bind directly the persons for whom they are made.[31] It was said that he could make only territorial laws, that is, laws which bind by reason of territorial subjection. It is now agreed by authors [32] that the Code permits a bishop to enact both territorial and personal laws. It must be admitted that, although the extent of one's territory be limited, it may be necessary that the subjects of that territory conform to certain important obligations outside the diocese as well as in it. The power of the bishop to make personal laws is implied in canon 201 §3: "Nisi aliud ex rerum natura aut ex iure constet potestatem iurisdictionis voluntariam seu non iudicialem quis exercere potest etiam in proprium commodum aut extra territorium existens aut in subditum e territorio absentem." It is likewise implied in the words of canon 8 §2: "Lex non praesumitur personalis sed territorialis nisi aliud constet," since no distinction is made between general and particular law, and especially in canon 14 §1 1° where it is prescribed that *peregrini* are bound by the particular legislation of their own territory whenever the laws are personal. There can be no doubt about the power of the bishop to make personal laws. There is only one condition upon which the exercise of the power depends. According

[30] Cf. Van Hove, *De Legibus Ecclesiasticis*, pp. 167-168.

[31] Suarez, *De Legibus*, 1. III, c. 32, n. 3-4. This opinion was based for the most part on a declaration of Boniface VIII that a penalty inflicted by a bishop did not bind outside his territory. Cf. c. 2 *Ut animarum*, I, 2, in VI°.

[32] De Schepper, *Collationes Brugenses*, XXIII (1923), 199-203, 219-222; Michiels, *Normae Generales*, I, 307-313; Van Hove, *De Legibus Ecclesiasticis*, pp. 132-134; *Irish Ecclesiastical Record*, 5 series, XXVI (1930), 526-528.

to canon 8 §2 the presumption is that a law is territorial, and therefore the presumption of territoriality must be certainly removed before the law can be considered personal. The presumption will be destroyed whenever the nature of the object of the obligation makes the law personal or when the transgression of the law causes a damage in one's own diocese (*nocet in proprio territorio*), as for example the law of residence. Besides, the bishop may remove the presumption by expressly making other obligations personal, except when the law is territorial by its nature or by common law. In practice, in order to remove all doubt, the personality of a law is best explicitly stated.

3. *Laws for Peregrini*

A most important question is the power of the bishop over *peregrini*, that is, those who are subjects of another diocese because of a domicile or quasi-domicile there but who actually are within his territory. It seems clear that he cannot legislate for them as he would for his own subjects.[33] On the other hand circumstances may demand that *peregrini* be obliged to conform to certain laws of the diocese. Therefore, in addition to the instances in which the Code expressly grants power over *peregrini*,[34] canon 14 §1 2° sets forth a general principle to govern the other possible cases: "[Peregrini adstringuntur] . . . neque legibus territorii in quo versantur iis exceptis quae ordini publico consulunt vel actuum solemnia determinant." The older canonists gradually came to accept this principle, so that just previous to the Code it was commonly held.[35] In the Code this norm has been for the first time imposed directly by the legislator.

With regard to obliging *peregrini* to observe the solemnities prescribed for certain acts there is no difficulty. It follows from the long accepted principle: "*Locus regit actum.*" Whatever is partic-

[33] Maroto (*Institutiones Juris Canonici*, I, 213, note 2) and Cicognani (*Jus Canonicum*, II, 104) maintain that the legislator can determine under what conditions *peregrini* may remain and act in a territory and that, unless they wish to observe the regulations, they cannot remain or act. This norm seems contrary to the principle of canon 14 §1 2°.

[34] Cc. 144, 804 §3, 1251, 2269 §2. Cf. S. C. Conc., 15 Nov. 1924—*Il Monitore Ecclesiastico*, XXXVII (1925), 106.

[35] Cf. Michiels, *Normae Generales*, I, 306.

ularly prescribed as the form of an act must be followed by everyone who performs the act in that territory. It is the phrase *quae ordini publico consulunt* that furnishes the real difficulty.

The public order cannot be equivalent to the common good which must be the purpose of all law. For then *peregrini* would be obliged by every law. Undoubtedly, therefore, it can only refer to laws which directly and immediately are intended for the good of the community as a whole, as distinguished from others which are directly for the benefit of the individual members and only mediately for the good of the entire community. In other words, it includes only the laws which are enacted that the society as such should be preserved and, moreover, have the means apt for attaining its end.[36] But even a greater restriction must be made because of the word *consulunt.* Thus, the phrase in the final analysis means all the laws that safeguard the public order, that is, those which are necessary if the proper public order is to exist. It embraces whatever laws are necessary in order to prevent what of its nature destroys public order. More specifically the phrase includes either the laws the transgression of which results in a real damage to the place where the *peregrini* are [37] or those which because of peculiar circumstances are absolutely necessary for the general good.[38] This is the interpretation that Van Hove,[39] elaborating the previous teaching of Vermeersch,[40] has given after a study of the opinions of the older

[36] Van Hove (*Ephemerides Theologicae Lovaniensis,* I (1924), 156-57), cites examples of laws of the public and private order in the Code. Canon 708 ordaining the formal erection of a confraternity is a law of public order, while canon 1684 prescribing the rescindibility of an act or contract under certain conditions is a law of the private order.

[37] ". . . quarum transgressio cederet in damnum et iniuriam illius loci in quo peregrini morantur"—St. Alphonsus, *Theologis Moralis,* I, Tract. 2, de legibus, n. 160.

[38] ". . . (peregrinos) obligari legibus etiam particularibus loci, si illae specialiter latae sunt in bonum illius loci ob necessitatem reipublicae . . ."—Schmalzgrueber, *Jus Ecclesiasticum Universum,* I, t. 2, n. 42.

[39] *Ephemerides Theologicae Lovaniensis,* I (1924), 153-158; *De Legibus Ecclesiasticis,* pp. 219-221.

[40] "Dici fortasse possit ordini publico consuli per eas leges quae ad commune damnum avertendum potius quam ad promovendum bonum commune latae sunt"—*Epitome,* I, 63.

canonists. It seems preferable to the other interpretations which have been advanced.[41]

According to Van Hove [42] and Michiels [43] the following may be considered particular instances of laws to which *peregrini* can be subjected: laws which concern public offices and the exercise of public authority; which directly rule the external public order as, for example, public processions or the order in church; which regard the dominion of things in that territory according to competence by reason of the location of the object in dispute (*res sita*); [44] which forbid acts that actually give scandal; which lay down regulations concerning clerical life.[45] There can be, of course, no complete list. But briefly whatever is prescribed as obliging *peregrini* must be for the safeguarding of the public order *per se* and by its nature. The power of the legislator as far as *peregrini* are concerned does not extend to the particular instances when *per accidens* the public order is disturbed.

A word must be said about the power of the bishop to make penal laws for *peregrini*. Because of the different views which are taken with regard to the nature of ecclesiastical penalties, there is a diversity of opinion on this question. Some [46] consider all punishment as directed for the protection of the public order with the consequence that *peregrini* are always bound by penal laws. Another opinion is that, since according to the words of canon 2286 vindicative penalties are for the public order ". . . directe ad delicti expiationem . . .",

[41] ". . . quae videlicet latae sunt ad delicta provenienda aut punienda . . ."—Toso, *Commentaria Minora*, I, 40; ". . . illae latae fuerunt ad praecavendum a delictis, eaque poenis prosequenda . . ."—Cicognani, *Jus Canonicum*, II, 103.

[42] *Ephemerides Theologicae Lovaniensis*, I (1924), 158-161; *De Legibus Ecclesiasticis*, pp. 221-222.

[43] *Normae Generales*, I, 319-322.

[44] C. 4 X, *de foro competenti*, II, 2.

[45] Cf. Decretum Vicariatus Urbis, 25 May 1918—*A. A. S.*, X (1918), 300; Decretum S. C. Consist., 30 Dec. 1918—*A. A. S.*, XI (1919), 39-43; Litterae Circulares S. C. Concilii, 1 July 1926—*A. A. S.*, XVIII (1926), 312; Teodori, "Peregrini quoad censuras," *Appolinaris*, IV (1931), 141.

[46] Maroto, *Institutiones Juris Canonici*, I, 209; Cicognani, *Jus Canonicum*, II, 103; Toso, *Commentaria Minora*, I, 40. The argument drawn from canon 1566 which states the competence of the forum *ratione delicti* in no way proves the legislative power to establish delicts for *peregrini*.

these by their nature always oblige *peregrini,* but that medicinal penalties do not since according to canon 2241 §1 they are directly ordained for the correction of the delinquent. A third opinion maintains that all penal laws in the Church are directed primarily for the reform of wrongdoers and have only accessorily the social character of preventing similar delicts among others. The spiritual good of the individual, according to this opinion, is not the exclusive end of ecclesiastical penalties but it is their principal end.[47] The Code has not settled the controversy, and therefore in practice it is impossible for a bishop to subject *peregrini* to all penal laws, since it is not certain that they must always be enacted to maintain the public order. However, it must be insisted that the principle of canon 2226 §1: "Poenae annexae legi aut praecepto obnoxius est qui lege aut praecepto tenetur nisi expresse eximatur" allows a bishop to bind *peregrini* expressly by penal sanctions which are to be added to a particular law demanded for the preservation of the public order. For in that case, since *peregrini* are bound by the command or prohibition, they can be obliged by the penalty which is considered accessorily and secondarily as a further safeguard for the public order.[48] Likewise they can be obliged by particular penal law added to higher laws which are enacted to preserve the public order.[49] In all other instances *peregrini* cannot be obliged by penal statutes.

4. *Laws for Orientals*

In a diocese in which there are a notable number of members of the Oriental rites united with the Latin rite a bishop may wish to include certain prescriptions concerning them in the synodal statutes. Michiels [50] states the general principle that Orientals may be bound by laws which are of such a nature that their purpose cannot be at-

[47] Lega, *Praelectiones Juris Canonici,* De delictis et poenis, p. 8.

[48] Vermeersch-Creusen, *Epitome,* I, 63; Van Hove, *Ephemerides Theologiae Lovaniensis,* I (1924), 165; Cappello, *De Censuris,* p. 21.

[49] Thus S. C. Conc. (*A. A. S.,* XVIII [1926], 312-313) pointed out to Ordinaries that they could threaten priests from other dioceses with *ipso facto* suspension when the priests were living in the dioceses of the Ordinaries in a way that was unbecoming to their state of life.

[50] *Normae Generales,* I, 45.

tained unless the Orientals are also obliged according to the norm given in canon 1: "Licet in Codice iuris canonici Ecclesiae quoque Orientalis disciplina saepe referatur, ipse tamen unam respicit Latinam Ecclesiam, neque Orientalem obligat, nisi de iis agatur, quae ex ipsa rei natura etiam Orientalem afficiunt." Consequently authors [51] agree that, according to canon 14 §1 2° Orientals can be bound like *peregrini* to observe the particular laws of a territory when the laws determine the solemnity of acts or are intended to safeguard the public order. Synodal statutes for the Orientals can be enacted according to the principles already indicated.

[51] Maroto, *Institutiones Juris Canonici*, I, 208-209; Cicognani, *Jus Canonicum*, II, 13; Duskie, *Canonical Status of Orientals in the United States*, p. 64; Michiels, *Normae Generales*, I, 45; Van Hove, *De Legibus Ecclesiasticis*, p. 9.

CHAPTER VIII

CELEBRATION OF THE SYNOD

Canon 357. § 1. Synodum dioecesanam convocat eique praeest Episcopus, non autem Vicarius Generalis sine mandato speciali nec Vicarius Capitularis.

Canon 1406. § 1. Obligatione emittendi professionem fidei, secundum formulam a Sede Apostolica probatam, tenentur:

1°. Coram praeside eiusve delegato, qui Oecumenico vel particulari Concilio aut Synodo dioecesanae intersunt cum voto seu consultivo seu deliberativo; praeses autem coram eodem Concilio vel Synodo;

Canon 362. Unicus est in Synodo legislator Episcopus, ceteris votum tantum consultivum habentibus; unus ipse subscribit synodalibus constitutionibus; quae, si in Synodo promulgentur, eo ipso obligare incipiunt, nisi aliud expresse caveatur.

Canon 385. § 1. In quavis dioecesi habeantur examinatores synodales et parochi consultores qui omnes in Synodo constituantur, propositi ab Episcopo, a Synodo approbati.

Canon 1574. § 1. In qualibet dioecesi presbyteri probatae vitae et in iure canonico periti, etsi extradioecesani, non plures quam duodecim eligantur ut potestate ab Episcopo delegata in litibus iudicandis partem habeant; quibus nomen esto iudicium synodalium aut pro-synodalium, si extra Synodum constituuntur.

§ 2. Quod ad eorum electionem, substitutionem, cessationem aut remotionem a munere attinet, serventur praescripta can. 385-388.

THE actual celebration of the synod is mostly a liturgical function and therefore details are not given in the Code. Both the *Pon-*

tificale Romanum[1] and the *Caeremoniale Episcoporum*[2] furnish the necessary directions for the proper liturgical preparation and celebration of the synod. The plan given is arranged that the synod continue for three sessions. There is, however, no obligation to prolong the synod, if the matters that are to be settled can be taken care of in fewer sessions. Authors[3] agree that a greater or lesser number of sessions may be held according as the needs of the diocese demand. As a result the prescriptions of the Pontifical will have to be adapted and arranged according to the number of sessions that are to be held.

The principal canonical prescription for the celebration of the synod is stated in canon 357 §1 to the effect that the bishop, and not the vicar capitular nor the vicar general without a special mandate, can preside over the synod. The term *episcopus*, however, is to be understood as including besides the residential bishop all who can convoke the synod; namely, abbots and prelates *nullius*, vicars and prefects apostolic, perpetual apostolic administrators, coadjutor bishops given to a bishop who is totally incapacitated, and pro-vicars and pro-prefects apostolic when the vicariate and prefecture are vacant. These alone have the right to preside over the synod when it is held in their territory and no one else may do so without their consent even if the synod were convoked legitimately. Of course, since the obligation to hold the synod is stated impersonally, any of these are perfectly free to delegate another to preside over the synod when he cannot assist at it personally. Canon 199 §1 permits an act of ordinary jurisdiction to be delegated to another.

There are four other points of canonical import which must be considered; namely, the order of precedence, the profession of faith, the enactment of the synodal legislation, and the approbation of officials to be chosen in the synod. The following four articles will treat of these matters.

[1] Part III, *Ordo ad Synodum.*

[2] Part I, c. XXXI.

[3] Bouix, *De Episcopo,* II, 379; Wernz, *Jus Decretalium,* II b, 739; Cappello, *De Visitatione Liminum,* I, 314; Vito, *Il Sinodo Diocesano,* p. 49, note 3.

Article I. Order of Precedence in the Synod

Arrangement of precedence among members of the synod for the processions and the order of seating in the preparatory and solemn sessions must be attended to beforehand. It is the mind of the Church that due deference and recognition be given according to one's position in its hierarchical organization, or the position of the one who is represented. Consequently the law is careful to lay down precise and exact norms which are to govern the right of one to precede another according to the honor and dignity of one's status. The rules which are given in various parts of the Code are the general criteria. They do not preclude the possibility of local custom or particular law making more definite prescriptions when the need arises.[4]

Bishop. There can be no doubt that as a consequence of his right to preside over the synod and because of the principle that whoever has authority over persons has the right of precedence over them,[5] the bishop or those who have a similar right to convoke the synod will precede all members of the synod. And in the event that a delegate presides in his stead the delegate will enjoy the precedence of the bishop.[6]

Coadjutor or Auxiliary Bishop. If in a diocese there is another bishop besides the residential bishop he enjoys the next place, because of the principle of canon 106 3°: "Inter diversas personas ecclesiasticas quarum nulla habeat in alias auctoritatem: qui ad gradum potiorem pertinent, praecedunt eis qui sunt inferioris gradus; . . ." Even when the bishop is not the vicar general according to canon 370 §1 he retains precedence over all the clergy.

Vicar General. The Code states clearly in canon 370 §1 that the vicar general ordinarily has precedence over all clerics of the

[4] C. 106 6°.

[5] C. 106 2°—"Cui est auctoritas in personas sive physicas sive morales eidem ius est praecedentiae supra illas."

[6] C. 106 1°—"Qui alius personam gerit ex eadem obtinet praecedentiam; sed qui in Conciliis aliisque similibus conventibus procuratorio nomine intersunt, sedent post illos ejusdem gradus qui intersunt nomine proprio; . . ."

diocese, even over those who are in dignities and over the members of the cathedral chapter. As Vito[7] points out, there is a twofold reason for the precedence of the vicar general. One reason is that, since juridically he is one person with the bishop, according to canon 106 1° he should have the precedence of the bishop; and the other is that, since he has authority over all persons in the diocese, according to canon 106 2° he should precede these. The only exception allowed by this canon is when one of the clergy is a bishop and the vicar general is not. Then the bishop will enjoy precedence. The same right of precedence apparently would not belong to the vicar delegate in the synods of vicariates and prefectures apostolic, because it was not explicitly conceded,[8] nor to the pro-vicar or pro-prefect when the government of the territory is not vacant, because of the silence of canon 309.

Cathedral Chapter. According to previous decisions of the Sacred Congregations of Rites[9] the cathedral chapter as a moral person had precedence over collegiate chapters and all clerics of the diocese including pastors. Canon 408 §1 renews the right which the cathedral chapter has to precede the collegiate chapter even in the church of the collegiate chapter, and canon 491 §2 lays down their right to precede religious in every place in the diocese.

With regard to precedence among the members of the chapter, the following rules are to be observed:

1. In the chapters in which there are prebends, according to canon 408 §2 the precedence is according to prebends—presbyteral, diaconal and subdiaconal—regardless of what are orders of the individual members.[10] Within the same prebend precedence depends not upon the time of one's admission into the chapter but upon the time when one was admitted to the prebend.

2. In other chapters, according to canon 408 §1 the order of precedence is as follows: those in dignity according to their estab-

[7] *Note Canonichi sulla Precedenza*, p. 17.

[8] Cf. S. C. de Prop., 8 Dec. 1919—*A. A. S.*, XII (1920), 120; Winslow, *Vicars and Prefects Apostolic*, pp. 71-72.

[9] *S. R. C.*, 7 May 1639—*Decreta Authentica*, n. 676; *S. R. C.*, 28 April 1703 ad 3—*Decreta Authentica*, n. 2112.

[10] Vito, *Note Canonichi sulla Precedenza*, p. 36.

lished order, then the ordinary canons according to the time of the possession of their office, then the titular canons followed by the honorary and beneficiary canons respectively. There are only two exceptions. A bishop has precedence over all priests, regardless of the time of his entrance into the chapter; priests precede members who are not priests.[11]

Klekotka [12] insists that the board of consultors have the right of precedence of the cathedral chapter. He admits that no express declaration is made in the Code concerning the matter. But he argues that since the principal duty of serving as the advisory council of the bishop is common to both, the same precedence should be equally enjoyed. Since this argument is not conclusive, a bishop would do well to grant the right of precedence to the consultors unless it is already enjoyed by reason of a legal custom.

Rector of the Seminary. Muniz [13] regards the order of canon 358 §1 with regard to the clergy who must be called to the synod as indicative of the precedence that must be given them. There is not, however, any positive reason in the Code to support his deduction. Consequently the rector of the seminary cannot demand precedence after the chapter or consultors. It has been decided that a seminary as a body has precedence immediately after the cross of the cathedral chapter.[14] Perhaps, therefore, the precedence due the seminary belongs to the rector, since according to canon 1368, he is the pastor. However, the question is doubtful and it is better that the bishop make some provision in the matter.

Representative of the Collegiate Chapter. According to the principle of canon 106 1° "Qui alius personam gerit, ex eadem obtinet praecedentiam," the representatives of the different collegiate chapters are to be given the precedence that is due the chapter which each one represents. This will be as follows:

1. The chapters which are considered *insignis* precede the others.
2. Among chapters of equal rank the precedence will be given

[11] Cf. Vito, *Note Canonichi sulla Precedenza*, p. 37.

[12] *Diocesan Consultors*, pp. 94-96.

[13] *Procedimientos*, I, 499.

[14] *Decreta Authentica S. C. Rituum*, n. 2126, 2233, 2641.

to the one who has always enjoyed it and, if that cannot be ascertained, to the one which existed first in the diocese.[15]

In case a bishop summons all the canons of the collegiate chapters to the synod, the precedence is determined by the rules given for the canons of the cathedral chapter.

VICARS FORANE. The only determination of the Code with regard to the right of precedence of forane vicars is that according to canon 450 §2 the vicar forane precedes all pastors and other priests of his district. Nothing is said about his precedence over the clergy who are not of his district. A bishop may establish this right of precedence according to canon 106 6°, if a legitimate custom does not already exist. But precedence cannot be given over the collegiate chapters.[16] The precedence of the vicars forane among themselves will be according to their dignity; and if of equal dignity, to the time of their ordination; and if ordained at the same time, according to their age.[17]

DIOCESAN PRIESTS. The following may be given as summarized rules for precedence among the clergy of the diocese:

1. All minor prelates according to their rank and the date of their appointment have precedence over all other priests of the diocese.[18]

2. According to canon 106 3° pastors have precedence over the other diocesan priests since they are of a higher grade. Among themselves the precedence is as follows: (a) According to canon 478 §1 the pastor of the Cathedral church has precedence. (b) The precedence among the other pastors is to be determined by the date of their induction as pastor, or, if that is the same time, the date of their ordination, or, if that is also the same, by seniority of age.[19] (c) Administrators of a parish are to have the precedence due the parish.[20] (d) By reason of canon 106 6° a bishop is able

[15] C. 106 5°. Cf. Vito, *Note Canonichi sulla Precedenza*, p. 11.

[16] Cf. Vito, *Note Canonichi sulla Precedenza*, p. 49.

[17] C. 106 3°.

[18] Cf. Vito, *Note Canonichi sulla Precedenza*, p. 26, note 1.

[19] C. 106 3°.

[20] Cc. 478 §1, 106 1°; cf. Fanfani, *De Jure Parochorum*, p. 349.

to lay down more definite norms of precedence, as for example the right of the pastors of city parishes to precede the pastors of rural parishes.[21]

3. The rest of the clergy will be arranged according to canon 106 3°. Precedence among them will be determined respectively by rank, orders, time of ordination and age.

Religious Superiors. Since the synod is seldom held in the church of a religious institute, the secular clergy will usually precede all religious superiors. Canon 491 §2 grants to the secular clergy precedence over religious outside the church of the institute. However, if the synod is celebrated in the church of a religious institute the superiors of that religion are to precede the secular clergy who are not members of the cathedral or collegiate chapters. The precedence of the superiors of the other institutes is unchanged.

Because the superiors represent their institutes at the synod they are to be given the precedence of the institute. The abbots of the monasteries, therefore, are to be arranged according to the precedence which their monasteries have always enjoyed or, if that is not known, according to the time they have existed in the diocese.[22] The superiors of the clerical religious will follow the same arrangement, except that the superiors of the orders will precede those from congregations.[23]

Article II. Profession of Faith

According to canon 1406 §1 1° the profession of faith is to be made in each diocesan synod both by the one who is presiding, whether it be the bishop or a delegate, and by all who are attending the synod with the right to vote. This must be regarded as a strict obligation that continues to bind until it is fulfilled,[24] against which no custom of any kind can ever have legal value.[25] Although the obligation of the profession must still be considered as primarily

[21] Cf. Vito, *Note Canonichi sulla Precedenza*, p. 43.
[22] C. 106 5°.
[23] C. 491 §1.
[24] Cf. Cocchi, *Commentarium in Codicem*, l. III, part 4, p. 180.
[25] C. 1408 taken with canon 5.

obliging the superors as it did formerly,[26] it is also directly imposed on each one who must make it. Moreover any who culpably fail to make the profession at the synod according to canon 2403 can be punished, in case of contumacy after a warning, by privation of their office, benefice, dignity or position.

The following directions are to be observed for the making of the profession of faith in the synod:

1. The Code makes no requirement as to the session of the synod in which the profession must be made. But the Pontifical places the time for it at the end of the first solemn session, and this should be observed. Magnin [27] and Pistocchi [28] maintain that, since the preparatory sessions are a part of the synod, the profession must be made in the first of these gatherings; while Vito,[29] although not considering this obligatory, believes that it could be done. It seems, more correct, however, to follow the directions of the Pontifical, whose liturgical prescriptions according to canon 2 have not been repealed by the Code.

2. The only formula to be used is the one approved by the Holy See and found in the present editions of the Code, and in the Roman Pontifical.[30]

3. Everyone must make the profession personally. If made by proxy, it is invalid.[31]

4. The president of the synod is to make it in the presence of the assembled members, and the members before the president or one who has been delegated to receive the profession.[32] Moreover, according to canon 1407 it is invalid when made before a lay person.

5. There is no need for each one to read the profession separately or even together with the others. It will suffice if, for example, the secretary of the synod or his assistant read it aloud in

[26] Cf. Vermeersch-Creusen, *Epitome*, II, 429; De Meester, *Compendium Juris Canonici*, III, part 1, p. 317; Cocchi, *Commentarium in Codicem*, l. III, part 4, p. 180.

[27] *Le Canoniste Contemporain*, XLVI (1924), 267.

[28] *De Synodo Dioecesana*, p. 47.

[29] *Il Sinodo Diocesano*, p. 51.

[30] C. 1406 §1.

[31] C. 1407.

[32] C. 1406 §1 1°.

the name of the rest. Then, when that has been done, each one in turn can place his hand on the book of the gospels and say the following words: "Sic juro, sic spondeo, sic me Deus adjuvet et haec sancta evangelia." [33]

There is no need for the members of the synod to take the anti-modernist oath. Mothon [34] because of the decision of the Holy Office on 22 March 1918 to the effect that although not mentioned in the Code the precautionary measures of Pius X against Modernism still oblige,[35] erroneously declares that the members who make the profession of faith at the synod must also take the oath. The previous regulations, however, make no mention of the oath being necessary for the members of the synod and therefore it cannot be considered as now obligatory.[36]

Article III. Enactment of the Synodal Legislation

1. *The Legislator of the Synod*

Since bishops are the successors of the Apostles and are by divine institution in charge of individual churches, which they rule with ordinary jurisdiction under the authority of the Roman Pontiff,[37] they enjoy legislative, judicial and coercive powers over their subjects within the limits assigned by the sacred canons.[38] The synod does not destroy or limit a bishop's legislative power. He can exercise it in the synod as well as outside it. Therefore, as has been pointed out previously, the members of the synod have not the right of deliberation as the members of the ecumenical, plenary, and provincial councils have. Their voice in the proceedings is only consultative, and thus may or may not be followed by the bishop.

[33] Cf. Cappello, *De Visitatione Liminum*, I, 317; De Meester, *Compendium Juris Canonici*, III, part 1, p. 317.

[34] *Institutions Canoniques*, I, p. 177, note 5; p. 178, note 9.

[35] *A. A. S.*, X (1918), 136.

[36] Motu Proprio *"Sacrorum Antistitum,"* 1 Sept. 1910 ad 7—*A. A. S.*, II (1910), 699; cf. also decisions of S. Consist. Cong. 25 Sept. 1910 ad 7—*ibid.* 741; 25 Oct. 1910—*ibid.* 856-857; 16 Dec. 1910—*ibid.* III (1911), 25.

[37] C. 329 §1.

[38] C. 335 §1.

In the past, and particularly in the eighteenth century, the contrary error that the clergy had a decisive vote in the synod was accepted in many places and caused frequent controversies.[39] Finally, in order to settle the matter, Pius VI in a constitution *"Auctorem fidei"* of August 28, 1794, condemned two propositions stating this error as taught by the heretical Synod of Pistoria of 1786.[40]

The Code in canon 362 has renewed the previously accepted principle that the bishop alone is the legislator in the synod. It is he who decides what is to be adopted.[41] It is expected that the bishop will take into account the suggestions that have been proffered; but in the final analysis he is free to accept or reject them as he sees fit. The only limitation of this power apart from the choice of the officials to be chosen in the synod is in relation to the matters for which the Code in other places requires the consent of the chapter or some commission.[42] For the synod does not change the juridical status of the bishop. Because he is the sole legislator, therefore, only the bishop subscribes to the synodal statutes. Not even the chapter or the board of consultors can claim a right to add their names. It is the exclusive right of the bishop.[43]

Canon 362 speaks of others having only a consultative vote. Must this be interpreted, therefore, as implying that the bishop is

[39] Cf. De Meester, *Compendium Juris Canonici,* I, 175-176; Magnin, *Le Canoniste Contemporain,* XLVI (1924), 257.

[40] "Doctrina quae statuit 'reformationem abusuum circa ecclesiasticam disciplinam in synodis dioecesanis ab episcopo et parochis aequaliter pendere et stabiliri debere ac sine libertate decisionis indebitam fore subjectionem suggestionibus et jussionibus episcoporum' (prop. ix): falsa, temeraria, episcopalis auctoritatis laesiva, regiminis hierarchii subversiva, favens haeresi Aerianae a Calvino innovatae. Item doctrina qua 'parochi aliive sacerdotes in Synodo congregati pronuntiantur una cum episcopo judices fieri, et simul innuitur, iudicium in causis fidei ipsis competere jure proprio et quidem etiam per ordinationem accepto' (prop. x): falsa, temeraria, ordinis hierarchii subversiva, detrahens firmitate definitionum judiciorumve dogmaticorum Ecclesiae, ad minus erronea"—*Fontes,* n. 475.

[41] Therefore the "placet" of the Roman Pontifical must be understood only as a consultative vote. Cf. Benedict XIV, *De Synodo Dioecesana,* 1. XIII, c. 1, n. 1; *S. C. C., Venetiarum,* 21 April 1592—*Fontes,* n. 2243.

[42] Cf. e. g. cc. 1532 §3, 1541 §2.

[43] Cf. Benedict XIV, *De Synodo Dioecesana,* 1. XIII, c. 2, n. 1.

obliged to consult the members of the synod in the solemn session in which he promulgates the statutes? Apparently that is not the intention of the legislator. From the text of the law it seems that the canon is only stating a general principle and not prescribing its observance at any particular time in the synod. Therefore, since the free discussions in the preparatory sessions, which are certainly obligatory as an integral part of the synod, will have given the members of the synod ample opportunty to voice their opinions and suggestions, another vote in the solemn sessions on the advisability of the statutes is unnecessary. However, the Roman Pontifical [44] prescribes the acceptance of the statutes by the clergy in the solemn session of the second day, and the Code has not changed in any way this liturgical prescription. It should therefore be observed, with all who have been convoked to the synod having the right to vote unless it was expressly denied in the invitation according to canon 358 §2. The voting can be regarded as a solemn ratification of what has already been accepted. However, because of the preparatory sessions another discussion need not precede.

Another question arises as to whether the bishop must obtain the counsel of the cathedral chapter or the board of consultors as a distinct unit from the synod before he promulgates the synodal statutes. There is no mention in the Code of the need of a special consultation. Therefore, a bishop is not obliged to consult the chapter or consultors unless a legitimate custom exists. However, if the statutes concern matters for which in other places the Code requires the advice of the chapter or consultors, it must be observed. The synod does not change the antecedent obligation. Moreover, in this instance it would not be correct to consider that the advice could be given by each member in the preparatory sessions. The chapter or board of consultors must be consulted as a distinct body.[45] Moreover, bishops of the United States are obliged by the

[44] Part III, Ordo ad Synodum (die secunda): ". . . Quo finito leguntur constitutiones per Synodum approbandae, quibus lectis, habito scrutinio, quae placent per Patres confirmantur . . ."

[45] The work of the chapter according to canon 391 §1 and 411 §1 and the terms of canon 427 "*coetus consultorum*" imply that their actions are to be those of a distinct group. Moreover, in the United States the Third Plenary

prescription of the Third Plenary Council of Baltimore[46] which require a bishop to obtain the advice of his consultors before promulgating the synodal legislation. This particular legislation is clearly *beside* the common law and therefore has not been abrogated by the Code. Of course on account of the required preparatory sessions there is less need for the consultors' advice now than there was before the Code. Nevertheless as an existing law it must be observed.[47]

2. *Promulgation of the Legislation*

It is clear from the words of canon 8 §1: "Leges instituuntur cum promulgantur" that it is necessary to promulgate the synodal statutes before they have the force of law.[48] An exact manner of promulgation has not been imposed, and therefore, according to canon 335 §2, the bishop is free to determine the mode. He may have them read publicly in the synod, or have them posted in a place especially for that purpose, or publish them in the diocesan newspaper. Of these, promulgation of the statutes in the synod is the usual way. Indeed it is much more solemn to promulgate the legislation in the assembly in which it has been adopted.[49] If there is synodal promulgation, it is not necessary to publish the statutes in other parts of the diocese, although usually provisions should be made by which statutes that concern the laity be published in some way outside the synod.[50] As soon as the statutes are promulgated, in whatever manner the bishop chooses, according to canons

Council of Baltimore has decreed: ". . . Consilium consultorum praestabitur collegialiter . . ."—*Acta et Decreta*, n. 21. Cf. Klekotka, *Diocesan Consultors*, p. 116.

[46] *Acta et Decreta*, n. 20.

[47] Kletkotka, *Diocesan Consultors*, p. 114.

[48] There is no need to submit the statutes to the Sacred Congregation of the Council for a review as is required by canon 291 §1 for the decrees of plenary and provincial councils. Cf. Benedict XIV, *De Synodo Dioecesana*, l. XIII, c. 3, n. 6.

[49] Magnin (*Le Canoniste Contemporain*, XLVI [1924] 269) notes that, if the bishop believes the statutes have not been formulated as exactly and definitely as they might be, nothing forbids him to postpone their promulgation until they have been rendered more exactly.

[50] Toso, *Commentaria Minora*, III, 194.

335 §1 and 362 they oblige immediately unless the bishop expressly permits a period of grace, which is to be computed according to the norm of canon 34 §3 2°.

3. *Obligation and Force of the Synodal Statutes*

Synodal statutes, since they are truly laws, oblige in conscience all for whom they have been made. The gravity of the obligation will depend on the importance of the matter for the private and common good, the intention of the legislator, and special circumstances.[51] The obligation of obedience exists only when in the framing of the statutes the bishop has observed the norms of common law and higher particular law and thus made laws only for those over whom he has authority and in regard to the matters about which he is competent. Otherwise the legislation is null and void. It is clear, however, that a bishop as legislator, or his successor, is perfectly free to dispense from any of these statutes.[52] Yet this should not be done at will and for any reason whatsoever. Even the bishop should regularly have a just and proportionate reason.[53]

The synodal statutes are *per se* perpetual. They cease to exist only when either the prescriptions becomes unjust or impossible to observe, or their purpose is no longer useful or obtainable,[54] or when they have been abrogated or derogated from by the law of a competent superior according to the norms of canon 22, or finally when a contrary legitimate custom has been established according to the norms of canon 27 §1. Until then the laws continue in force to be observed according to the authentic interpretation which only the bishop or his successor or delegate can give.[55] It is clear that if

[51] Cf. Van Hove, *De Legibus Ecclesiasticis,* pp. 145-146.

[52] C. 80. Moreover, the superior of the bishop or a duly authorized delegate has similar power.

[53] C. 84 §1: "A lege ecclesiastica ne dispensetur sine iusta et rationabili causa, habita ratione gravitatis legis a qua dispensatur; alias dispensatio ab inferiore data illicita et invalida est." Cf. Michiels, *Normae Generales,* II, 499.

[54] Cf. Michiels, *Normae Generales,* I, 486-488; Van Hove, *De Legibus Ecclesiasticis,* pp. 346-348.

[55] C. 17 §1.

anyone feels that there is an unjust law included in the statutes recourse may be had to the Sacred Congregation of the Council.[56] However, the recourse does not suspend the obligation to abide by the statutes until the Holy See has settled the controversy (*in devolutivo*).

Article IV. Approbation of Officials in the Synod

The Code in several canons prescribes that certain of the diocesan officials be ordinarily selected in the synod, namely, synodal examiners, parish priest consultors, and synodal judges.

1. *Synodal Examiners*

According to canon 385 §1 each diocese regardless of its size should have a certain number of synodal examiners who will take charge of clerical examinations and participate in the different administrative processes concerning the clergy.[57] Likewise, these officials must be appointed in abbeys or prelatures *nullius* which have at least three canonical parishes.[58] But it does not appear that a similar obligation exists for vicariates and prefectures apostolic, since the Code is silent on the point; although Vromant [59] maintains that even there synodal examiners must be chosen. The regular place for the selection of these officials is in the synod. According to canon 387 §1 those who are in office even though they have not held it for ten years *ipso facto* lose it when the synod is celebrated, with the result that they cannot exercise their duties validly after the synod unless in regard to a matter which they had taken up before the synod began. It is important, therefore, to give consideration to the choice of synodal examiners as the time for the synod approaches.

The number of synodal examiners will be best determined by the needs of the diocese. According to canon 385 §2 the minimum

[56] Cf. Const. Leo XIII *"Romanos Pontifices,"* 8 May 1881, n. 13—*Fontes*, n. 582; Benedict XIV, *De Synodo Dioecesana*, l. XIII, c. 5, n. 13.

[57] Cc. 130, 389, 459 §3 3°, 2144, 2148, 2159, 2162, 2168, 2176, 2182.

[58] Cf. cc. 215 §2, 319 §2.

[59] *Jus Missionariorum*, p. 241, note 2.

number is to be four and the maximum twelve. It is the right of the bishop to select suitable candidates for these offices without any obligation to seek the advice of the chapter or consultors. He should select a sufficient number to give the clergy in the synod an opportunity to reject whom they do not want; and, if they are not satisfied with those named, he is obliged to submit the names of others.[60] In other words, the clergy should have absolute freedom in their choice. The candidates selected by the bishop, besides being morally above reproach, should be well versed in theology and canon law in order that they may carry out the duties of their office.[61] Nothing forbids that among this number be included some parish priests. However, the pastors who act as parish priest consultors ought not be appointed synodal examiners.[62] Moreover, it is desirable that the Vicar General should not hold the office of examiner.[63] Outside of these requirements the bishop is free to propose any of the diocesan priests and even a religious or a secular from outside the diocese.

The Code gives the clergy of the synod the right of deliberation in the selection of examiners from these candidates; and therefore, if this is not observed, according to canon 105 1° the choice of the examiners in the synod is invalid. However, the deliberative right of the clergy is called an approbation and, therefore, it need not be considered as a strict canonical election to be carried out according to the norms laid down in canons 160-178.[64] It seems sufficient to announce the names of the candidates in the preparatory session so that the clergy, if they wish, can present their objections against the ones who are proposed. Then the bishop may take from the list of candidates against whom no serious objection has been made the number of examiners that are to be appointed. The selection may be ratified by all the clergy in a public vote at the end of the first solemn session of the synod as the Pontifical arranges. However, if it is thought advisable, a secret written ballot may be

[60] Benedict XIV, *De Synodo Dioecesana*, 1. IV, c. 7, n. 3; Bouix, *De Episcopo*, I, 373.

[61] S. Cong. Studiorum, 7 March 1907—*A. S. S.*, XL (1907), 380.

[62] S. C. Consist., 3 Oct. 1910, ad 4, 5, 7, 8—*Fontes*, 2076.

[63] S. C. Consist., 3 Oct. 1910, ad 6—*Fontes*, 2076.

[64] Muniz, *Procedimientos*, I, 94.

arranged. An alphabetical list of the names and surnames of the candidates should be given to each of the clergy who has the right to vote. Some authors [65] maintain that the approbation is to be decided according to canon 101, that is, that an absolute majority is required on either the first two ballots or that in the third ballot a relative majority suffices. But since the synod is not a collegiate moral person, there is no need to follow this method. It is enough, according to canon 105 2°, that the candidates who receive the greater number of votes of the members be considered the choice of the synod.[66]

Immediately after the approbation of the examiners has taken place in the solemn session of the synod the Pontifical prescribes that those chosen are to make an oath in the hands of the bishop. Here, then, though it is not obligatory, they may take the oath required by canon 364 §2 1° that they will exercise their office faithfully. The anti-modernistic oath can also be taken at this time.[67]

2. *Parish Priest Consultors*

The second group of diocesan officials to be chosen in the synod are parish priest consultors, who also intervene in certain administrative processes affecting the clergy.[68] Apart from the fact that, as their name denotes, they must always be pastors or at least parochial vicars,[69] the qualities demanded in these officials are the same as for synodal examiners. They likewise are to be designated by the bishop and approved by the clergy of the synod, as the examiners, and afterwards they may there take the oath to carry out the duties of their office faithfully and the anti-modernistic oath.

[65] Maroto, *Institutiones Juris Canonici,* I, 728; Wernz-Vidal, *De Personis,* p. 696; Coronata, *Institutiones Juris Canonici,* I, 495, note 6.

[66] Vermeersch-Creusen, *Epitome,* I, 252; Vito, *Il Sinodo Diocesano,* p. 61, note 2.

[67] S. Consist. Cong., 25 Sept. 1910, ad 7—*A. A. S.,* II (1910), 741.

[68] Cf. cc. 2144 §1, 2153 §1, 2154 §1, 2165.

[69] S. C. Consist., 3 Oct. 1910, ad 4—*Fontes,* n. 2076. According to this decision a religious as long as he was a pastor could act in this capacity.

3. *Synodal Judges*

The third group of officials to be approved in the synod are synodal judges. These officials are to be selected for the diocesan collegiate tribunal and, when there is only one judge, to act at times as consulting assessors.[70] The same manner of selecting the synodal judges is to be used as for synodal examiners. It is true that canon 1574 §2 speaks of their election. But it seems that the word is used only as a generic term and need not be taken in its strict canonical sense. Because reference is expressly made to the section of the Code on synodal examiners, it cannot be interpreted as changing to any extent what is there laid down.

The number of the synodal judges will depend upon the needs of the diocese. In canon 1574 §1 it is explicitly said that there should be no more than twelve, but, unlike the statement for synodal examiners, no minimum is given. However, there should be at least four in order to constitute with the *officialis* the tribunal of five required by canon 1576 §1 2°. The ones designated by the bishop should be priests, [71] of blameless conduct and well versed in canon law. Extradiocesan priests are explicitly included as possible candidates. Noval [72] insists that religious should not be appointed as synodal judges. In support of his opinion, he refers to canon 626, which states that religious should not engage themselves in anything incompatible with the religious state. But as Roberti [73] points out, the duties of the office will not entirely absorb the activity of religious. Accordingly the appointment of the religious to this office is not contrary to canon 626.[74] This opinion, therefore, can be followed in practice.

After the judges have been approved in the synod, as members of the curia they may take the oath to carry out their duties faithfully, as well as the anti-modernistic oath.

[70] C. 1574 §1, 1575.

[71] Blat (*Commentarium Codicis,* IV, 45) insists that this requirement of the Code would exclude titular bishops. But it would seem that this is stating only the minimum and not excluding those of a higher order.

[72] *De Processibus,* p. 63.

[73] *De Processibus,* I, 171.

[74] Cf. Schäfer, *De Religiosis.*

APPENDIX

THE following letter of announcement of the synod is suggested as a model. Necessary formulas can be found in *Praxis Synodalis*, pp. 66 ff. and Bouix's *De Episcopo*, II, 413 ff.

To the Clergy of the Diocese of ——————:

Some time in the course of the present year a Diocesan Synod will be held in the Cathedral City in which legislation for the welfare of the Church in this Diocese is to be enacted.

The exact time for the holding of the Synod will be settled as soon as a survey of preliminary committee work permits of a designation.

As one of the most necessary preparations for the Synod is the Invocation of Divine Help, we hereby ordain that the *Oratio De Spiritu Sancto* be added to the Mass every Monday, Rubrics permitting.

The Faithful shall likewise be asked by the Priests to pray for the success of the Synodal Legislation.

The following members of the Clergy have been appointed officials of the Synod:

PROMOTER OF SYNOD— ....

PROCURATOR OF CLERGY— ....

GENERAL SECRETARY— ....

NOTARY— ....

The Committees herein mentioned are hereby appointed to consider and draft for Synodal enactment the various matters of Legislation submitted by the Promoter of the Synod and such other subjects as the Secular and the Religious Clergy of the Diocese desire to submit through the Procurator of the Clergy. All members of the Secular and the Religious Clergy of the Diocese are asked to make such suggestions for legislative enactment as they deem necessary or useful for the welfare of the Diocese. The Procurator of the Clergy shall receive and forward to the respective Committees the suggestions submitted.

I. GENERAL COMMITTEE—Bishop, Vicar General, Consultors.

II. SPECIAL COMMITTEES

1. DE CURIA—Bishop, Vicar General, *Secretary*, N. ....
NN. ....
2. DE CLERICIS—*Chairman*, N. ...., *Secretary*,
N. .... NN. ....
3. DE LAICIS—*Chairman*, N. .... *Secretary*,
N. .... NN. ....

4. De Sacramentis—*Chairman,* N. .... *Secretary,* N. .... NN. ....
5. De Magisterio Ecclesiastico—*Chairman,* N. .... *Secretary,* N. .... NN. ....
6. De Temporalibus—*Chairman,* N. .... *Secretary,* N. .... NN. ....

The enclosed statement, prepared by the Promoter of the Synod at the direction and with the delegation of the Bishop, covers the materials and methods of procedure.

....

Bishop of ....

....

Chancellor

To the Clergy of the Diocese of ——————:

The subjects indicated on the following pages and other suggestions to be submitted later by the Clergy are to be discussed by the respective committees and drafted into brief legislative form.

The Committee-secretaries will send in to the General Secretary the drafts decided on by their Committees, and also minority reports, if so desired.

The General Secretary will submit the above to the Promoter of the Synod.

All Committees will meet on the First and Third Tuesdays from 10 A. M. until 1 P. M.

De Curia meets at Bishop's House, in ....
De Clericis meets at ...., in ....
De Laicis meets at Chancery Office, in ....
De Sacramentis meets at ...., in ....
De Magisterio meets at ...., in ....
De Temporalibus meets at ...., in ....

....

Promoter of Synod.

....

General Secretary.

I. Committee—*De Curia:*

a. Bishop. b. Vicar General. c. Chancellor. d. Judges. e. Officialis. f. Notaries. g. Suggested topics.

II. Committee—*De Clericis:*

a. Privilege of the Forum.

Canon 120 to be explicitated so as to forbid conflicts in Civil Courts between lay people and ecclesiastical corporations, parishes, convents, etc.; likewise to preclude Civil Court procedure by clerics against lay people, Catholic or non-Catholic, without permission of Bishop.

b. Priests should not act as jurors. c. Priests should consult with Ordinary before taking up civic activities. d. Retreats. e. Examinations. f. Conferences. g. Diocesan Consultors. h. Meetings and duties, also during vacancy of See. i. Deans. j. Pastors. k. Their appointment. Duties. Parish records. l. Assistants.

De Religiosis.

a. Urging vocations to religious life. b. Appointment of confessors Ordinary and Extraordinary. c. Chaplains for religious. d. Spiritual care of religious. Conferences. e. Cooperation between seculars and religious. f. Religious in charge of parishes. g. Financial statements when and where required.

Suggested Topics.

III. COMMITTEE—*De Laicis:*

a. Lay Organizations. b. Societies. c. Lay Apostolate. d. Lay interest in parochial and diocesan activities. e. Confraternities. f. Sodalities. g. Lay Retreats. h. Suggested topics.

IV. COMMITTEE—*De Sacramentis et Sacramentalibus. De Cultu Divino:*

Baptism.

a. Care concerning administration, registration. b. The proper instructions before baptism of adults. Care in selection of sponsors. Careless Catholics should not be admitted as sponsors. Place and time of baptism.

Confirmation.

a. Proper preparation of candidates. Also for ceremonies of Confirmation. b. Care as to sponsors. c. Registration. d. Confirmation of adults.

Holy Eucharist.

a. Care concerning materials—host—wine. b. Mass Stipends. c. Frequent and Daily Communion. d. Communion for the sick. e. Communion of children. Preparation for same. f. Easter duty of faithful.

Penance.

a. Faculties. b. Reserved cases. c. Confessionals. d. Indulgences.

Extreme Unction.

Care and instruction concerning same.

Holy Orders.

Regulations concerning candidates.

De Matrimonio.

a. Proper instructions. b. Publication of banns. c. Dispensation from Impediments. d. Mixed marriages. Instruction of non-Catholic party before same. e. Time—Place—Ceremonies of celebration of marriage. f. Separation of parties after marriage. g. Pauline Privilege. h. Efforts to validate invalid marriages. i. Presentation of petition for declaration of nullity to Ecclesiastical Courts. j. Registration of marriage.

Divine Worship.

a. Devotions. b. Vespers. c. Approved prayers. d. Care of altar. e. Vestments. f. Relics. g. Processions.

Suggested Topics.

V. Committee—*De Magisterio Ecclesiastico:*

a. Profession of Faith, When, Where, As official act. Canon 461 to be explicitated. b. Antimodernistic Oath cf. Vermeersch-Creusen Epitome, Vol. II, 3rd ed., p. 460. c. Defense and spread of Faith. d. Missions to Catholics and non-Catholics. e. Sermons, Course of Sermons. f. Catechetical instructions for children in Catholic schools. g. Catechetical instructions for children in non-Catholic schools. h. What can be done by priests to offset non-Catholic influence in Public Schools? In some places, priests gather the Catholic children that attend public schools and instruct them correctly on those points about which they have been misinformed. The Church is often placed in a false light by the teachers of history in public schools. The growing generation imbibes a false philosophy. There ought to be a concerted effort on the part of priests to offset all these wrong influences. i. Urging attendance at Catholic schools and colleges. j. Seminary. k. Vocations. l. Acquainting people with Encyclicals of Pope. m. Pastoral Letters. n. Support of Catholic press. Pamphlets. Books. o. Efforts for converts. Attention to same. p. Frequent warning in pulpit and in school against carelessness, indifference, in faith, against attendance at non-Catholic services, against reading of improper literature, carelessness concerning attendance at Mass. q. Suggested topics.

VI. Committee—*De Temporalibus:*

a. Churches and chapels. b. Permission to erect same. c. Shrines. d. Diocesan Building Commission. Its functions. e. Upkeep and repair of churches. f. Altars. Construction. g. Cemeteries, parochial, interparochial, mixed. h.

Funerals. Proper burials. Exhumation. Cremation. Refusal of burial. i. Observance of Sundays and Fast Days. j. Desecration. k. Fast and abstinence.

De Bonis Ecclesiae Temporalibus.

a. Regulations covering buying and location of church property. Lots, buildings, etc. b. Registration of deeds. Titles. c. Collections.

Administration of Church Property.

a. Relation to civil laws. b. Board of Administration. c. Insurance. d. Documents of Insurance, Mortgages, Leases, Sale.

Suggested Topics.

Since usually the practice in the United States is to hold the synod on one day, the following *Ordo ad Synodum* has been arranged. The essential parts of the *Ordo* given in the Roman Pontifical are included.

I.

Missa Solemnis Pontificalis
In honorem Spiritus Sancti

II.

Post Missam:

1. Antiphona: "Exaudi nos, Domine ...." (Pontificale Romanum, 62 ff.)
2. "Adsumus, Domine ...." (Pont. Rom., 65 f.)
3. "Omnipotens sempiterne Deus ...." (Pont. Rom., 66)
4. "Litaniae Omnium Sanctorum ...." (Pont. Rom., 15 ff.; Breviarium versus finem)
5. Flectamus genua. Levate. Oremus: "Da quaesumus ...." (Pont. Rom., 67)
6. Sequentia S. Evangelii sec. Lucam, c. ix (Pont. Rom., 67)
7. "Veni Creator Spiritus" (Pont. Rom., 68; Breviarium in Festo Pentecostes)
8. "Venerabiles consacerdotes ...." (Pont. Rom., 68)
9. Decretum de Synodo aperienda.
10. Leguntur nomina Officialium Synodi.
11. Professio Fidei. (Omnes genuflectunt)
    "Ego NN. .... curaturum." Postea omnes surgunt et dicunt: "Ego idem NN. spondeo, voveo ac iuro. Sic me Deus adiuvet et haec sancta Dei Evangelia."

12 Approbatio Judicum et Examinatorum Synodalium et Parochorum Consultorum.
13. Eorundem iusiurandum de officio adimplendo. (Iusiurandum antimodernisticum vel nunc vel postea.)
14. Statuta Synodalia. (selecta quaedam)
15. Decretum Promulgationis Statutorum Synodalium.
16. Oremus: "Nulla est ...." (Pont. Rom., 85)
(Deinde Pontifex solemniter omnibus benedicit, dicens: "Sit nomen Domini benedictum, etc."
17. "Recedamus cum pace"
(Et respondent omnes: "In nomine Christi.")

BIBLIOGRAPHY

Sources

Acta Apostolicae Sedis, Rome, 1909.

Acta Sanctae Sedis, 41 vols., Rome, 1865-1908.

Acta et Decreta Concilii Plenarii Americae Latinae, 2 vols., Rome, 1900.

Acta et Decreta Concilii Plenarii, Australensis III, Sydney, 1907.

Acta et Decreta Conciliorum Recentiorum (Collectio Lacensis), 7 vols., Freiburg in Breisgau, 1870-1890.

Caeremoniale Episcoporum, Mechlin, 1867.

Codex Juris Canonici, Rome, 1918.

Codicis Juris Canonici Fontes, cura Emi. Petri Card. Gasparri editi, 5 vols., Rome, 1925-1930.

Collectanea S. Congregationis de Propaganda Fide, 2 vols., Rome, 1907.

Concilii Plenarii Baltimorensis II, Acta et Decreta, Baltimore, 1868.

Concilii Plenarii Baltimorensis III, Acta et Decreta, Baltimore, 1886.

Corpus Juris Canonici (Richter-Friedberg), 2 vols., Leipzig, 1879.

Decreta Authentica Congregationis Sacrorum Rituum, 7 vols., Rome, 1898.

Hardouin, J., *Acta Conciliorum et Epistolae Decretales ac Constitutiones Summorum Pontificum*, 12 vols., Paris, 1715.

Mansi, J., *Sacrorum Conciliorum Nova et Amplissima Collectio*, 53 vols., Paris-Arnheim-Leipzig, 1901-1927.

Pontificale Romanum, 3 vols., Mechlin, 1855.

Theodosiani Libri XVI cum Constitutionibus Sirmondianis (Kreuger-Mommsen edition), 3 vols., Berlin, 1895.

Thesaurus Resolutionum S. Congregationis Concilii, 167 vols., Rome, 1718-1908.

Works of Reference

Aichner, S., *Compendium Juris Ecclesiastici*, Brescia, 1887.

Alzog, J., *Manual of Church History*, trans. by F. Pabisch, 5 vols., Cincinnati, 1874.

Annali del Seminario Giuridico della R. Università di Palermo, Vol. XIV, Cortona, 1930.

Ayrinhac, H., *Constitution of the Church in the New Code of Canon Law*, New York, 1925.

[Bachofen], Chas. Augustine, *A Commentary on the New Code of Canon Law*, 8 vols., St. Louis, 1921-1925.

—— *Rights and Duties of Ordinaries according to the Code and Apostolic Faculties*, St. Louis, 1924.

Bargilliat, M., *Praelectiones Juris Canonici,* 2 vols., Paris, 1921.

Bastnagel, C., *Appointment of Parochial Adjutants and Assistants,* Washington, 1930.

Batiffol, P., *Etudes d'Histoire et de Théologie Positive,* first series, Paris, 1926.

Bellarmine, R., *Opera Omnia,* editio nova juxta Venetam anni MDCCXXI, Eminentiss. Cardinali Xisto Riario Sforza dicata, Naples, 1872.

Benedict XIV, *De Synodo Dioecesana,* Venice, 1792.

Bingham, J., *Origines Ecclesiasticae,* or *Antiquities of the Christian Church,* 9 vols., London, 1844.

Blat, A., *Commentarium Textus Codicis Juris Canonici,* 6 vols., Rome, 1921-1927.

Bouix, D., *Tractatus de Capitulis,* Paris, 1872.

—— *Tractatus de Episcopo ubi et de Synodo Dioecesana,* 2 vols., Paris, 1859.

Brat, B., *Les Livres Pénitentiaux et La Pénitence Tarifée,* Brignais, 1910.

Calenzio, G., *Documenti Inediti e Nuovi Lavori Letterarii sul Concilio di Trento, Rome,* 1874.

Campagna, M., *Il Vicario Generale del Vescovo,* Washington, 1931.

Cappello, F., *De Censuris,* Turin, 1925.

—— *De Curia Romana,* 2 vols., Rome, 1911-1912.

—— *De Visitatione SS. Liminum et Dioeceseon,* 2 vols., Rome, 1912.

—— *Summa Juris Canonici,* Vol. I, Rome, 1928.

Catholic Encyclopedia, 17 vols., New York, 1907-1922.

Chelodi, J., *Jus de Personis,* Trent, 1927.

Choupin, L., *Valeur des Decisions Doctrinales et Disciplinaires du Saint Siege,* Paris, 1928.

Cicognani, H., *Jus Canonicum,* Rome, 1925.

—— *Commentarium ad Librum I Codicis,* Rome, 1925.

Claeys-Bouuaert, F., *De Canonica Cleri Saecularis Obedientia,* Louvain, 1904.

Coady, J., *Appointment of Pastors,* Washington, 1929.

Cocchi, G., *Commentarium in Codicem Juris Canonici,* 7 vols., Turin, 1925-1927.

Concilii Tridentini Diariorum, Actorum, Epistolarum, Tractatuum Nova Collectio, edidit Societas Goerresiana, 8 vols., Freiburg, 1901-30.

Coronata, M., *Institutiones Juris Canonici,* Vol. I, Turin, 1928.

—— *De Locis et Temporibus Sacris,* Turin, 1922.

Cox, J., *Administration of Seminaries,* Washington, 1931.

Craisson, D., *Manuale Totius Juris Canonici,* 4 vols., Poitiers, 1875.

Cunningham, D., *Historical Background of National Parishes,* Washington, 1930. [Not printed.]

D'Angelo, S., *La Curia Diocesana,* 2 vols., Giarre, 1922-1928.

—— *Parroco e Parrocchia,* 2 vols., Giarre, 1921-1923.

Dargin, E., *Reserved Cases,* Washington, 1924.

De Brabandere, A., *Juris Canonici et Juris Canonico-Civilis Compendium,* 2 vols., Bruges, 1866.

De Meester, A., *Juris Canonici et Juris Canonico-Civilis Compendium*, 3 vols., Bruges, 1921-1928.

Dictionnaire du Droit Canonique, 3 fasc., Paris, 1924-1928.

Dictionnaire de Théologie Catholique, 9 vols., Paris, 1903-1926.

Duchesne, L., *Early History of the Church*, New York, 1909.

Duskie, J., *Canonical Status of Orientals in the United States*, Washington, 1928.

Faciolati-Forcellini, *Lexicon Totius Latinitatis*, revised by Coredini, Perugia, 1887.

Fagnanus, P., *Commentaria in Quinque Libros Decretalium*, 4 vols., Venice, 1709.

Fanfani, L., *De Jure Parochorum ad Normam Codicis Juris Canonici*, Turin, Rome, 1924.

Ferraris, L., *Bibliotheca Canonica, Juridica, Moralis, Theologica, necnon Ascetica, Polemica, Rubricistica, Historica*, 8 vols., Rome, 1768.

Ferrerres, J., *Institutiones Canonicae*, 2 vols., Barcelona, 1920.

Fisher, J., *History of the Christian Church*, New York, 1893.

Golden, H., *Parochial Benefices in the New Code*, Washington, 1921.

Gothofredus, J., *Codex Theodosianus cum Perpetuis Commentariis*, 6 vols., Leipzig, 1743.

Gousset, *Exposition des Principes du Droit Canonique*, Paris, 1859.

Hatch, E., *Organization of the Early Christian Church*, London, 1918.

Hefele-Clark, *History of the Christian Councils*, 5 vols., Edinburg, 1883.

Hefele-Leclerque, *Histoire des Conciles*, 5 vols., Paris, 1910.

Hickey, J., *Irregularities and Simple Impediments*, Washington, 1920.

Klekotka, P., *Diocesan Consultors*, Washington, 1920.

Lega, M., *Praelectiones in Textus Juris Canonici.* De Delictis et Poenis. Rome, 1910.

Liddell-Scott, *Greek-English Lexicon*, New York, 1850.

Lightfoot, J., *Dissertations on the Apostolic Age*, London, 1892.

Ligouri, St. Alphonsus, *Theologia Moralis*, 4 vols., Turin, 1821.

McGuigan, J., *The Diocesan Synod*, Washington, 1927. [Not printed.]

Maroto, P., *Institutiones Juris Canonici*, Vol. I, Rome, 1921.

Michiels, M., *De Origine Episcopatus*, Louvain, 1900.

Michiels, G., *Normae Generales*, 2 vols., Dublin, 1929.

Migne, J., *Encyclopedie Theologique*, Series 1, 50 vols., Paris, 1847.

—— *Patrologiae Cursus Completus*, Series Graeca, 161 vols., Paris, 1857-1866.

—— *Patrologiae Cursus Completus*, Series Latina, 221 vols., Paris, 1844-1855.

Milman, J., *History of Christianity*, New York, 1841.

Monin, A., *De Curia Romana*, Louvain, 1912.

Moran, W., *Government of the Church in the First Century*, New York, 1913.

Mothon, J., *Institutions Canoniques*, 3 vols., Paris, 1922-1924.

Muniz, T., *Procedimientos Ecclesiasticos*, 3 vols., 2 ed., Seville.

Noval, J., *Commentarium Codicis Juris Canonici,* Vol. IV, De Processibus, Rome, 1920.

O'Connor, P., *Residence of Pastors,* Washington, 1930. [Not printed.]

Oesterle, G., *Praelectiones Juris Canonici,* Vol. I, Rome, 1931.

Ojetti, B., *Commentarium in Codicem Juris Canonici,* 2 vols., Rome, 1927-1928.

—— *Synopsis Rerum Moralium et Juris Pontificii,* 4 vols., Rome, 1909-1914.

Pallotini, S., *Collectio Omnium Conclusionum et Resolutionum quae in causis propositis apud S. Cong. Cardinalium S. Concilii Tridentini Interpretum prodierunt ab anno 1564 ad annum 1860,* 17 vols., Rome, 1868-1893.

Papp-Szilagyi, *Enchiridion Juris Ecclesiae Orientalis Catholicae,* Gran Varadino, 1880.

Phillips, G., *Die Diöcesansynode,* Freiburg, 1849.

—— *Compendium Juris Ecclesiastici,* Ratisbon, 1875.

Pickering, H., *Lexicon of the Greek Language,* Boston, 1846.

Pistocchi, M., *De Synodo Dioecesana,* Turin, 1922.

Praxis Synodalis, New York, 1883.

Reiffenstuel, A., *Jus Canonicum Universum,* 7 vols., Paris, 1864.

Richter-Schulte, *Canones et Decreta Concilii Tridentini,* Leipzig, 1853.

Roberti, F., *De Processibus,* 2 vols., Rome, 1926.

Santi, F., *Praelectiones Juris Canonici,* 2 vols., Ratisbon, 1886.

Schäfer, T., *De Religiosis,* Münster i. W., 1931.

Schaff, P., *History of the Christian Church,* 7 vols., New York, 1905.

Schmalzgrueber, F., *Jus Ecclesiasticum Universum,* 12 vols., Rome, 1843-1845.

Sole, J., *De Delictis et Poenis,* Rome, 1920.

Smith, S., *Elements of Ecclesiastical Law,* 2 vols., New York, 1883.

Studi in Onore di Biagio Brugi, Palermo, 1910.

Suarez, F., *Opera Omnia,* 23 vols., Paris, 1856.

Thomassinus, L., *Vetus et Nova Ecclesiae Disciplina circa Beneficia et Beneficiarios,* Mainz, 1787.

Toso, Al., *Commentaria Minora ad Codicem Juris Canonici,* vol. III, Rome, 1921.

Trombetta, A., *De Pallio Archiepiscopali,* Sorento, 1923.

Van Espen, Z., *Jus Ecclesiasticum Universum,* editio novissima Joannis Petri Gibert, 10 vols., Venice, 1769.

Van Hove, A., *Commentarium Lovaniense,* Vol. I, t. I, *Prolegomena ad Codicem Juris Canonici,* Mechlin, 1928, Vol. I, t. II, *De Legibus Ecclesiasticis,* Mechlin, 1930.

Veggian, T., *Il Sinodo Diocesano,* Vincenza, 1920.

Vermeersch-Creusen, *Epitome Juris Canonici,* 2 ed., 3 vols., Mechlin-Rome, 1925-1927.

Vito, P., *Il Sinodo Diocesano,* Naples, 1928.

—— *Note Canonichi sulla Precedenza,* Verona, 1924.

Vromant, G., *Jus Missionariorum,* Vol. II, *De Personis,* Louvain, Paris, Brussels, 1929.

Wernz, F., *Jus Decretalium,* 6 vols., Rome, 1906.
Wernz-Vidal, *Jus de Personis,* Rome, 1928.
Winslow, F., *Vicars and Prefects Apostolic,* Washington, 1924.
Zaplontik, J., *De Vicariis Foraneis,* Washington, 1923.
Ziegler, F., *Church and State in Visigothic Spain,* Washington, 1930.

PERIODICALS

Apollinaris, Rome, 1928—
Canoniste Contemporain (Le), Paris, 1878—
Collationes Brugenses, Bruges, 1900—
Ephemerides Theologicae Lovaniensis, Louvain, 1924—
Irish Ecclesiastical Record, The, Dublin, 1864—
Jus Pontificium, Rome, 1921—
Monitore Ècclesiastico (Il), Rome, 1875—
Periodica de re canonica et morali utili praesertim Religiosis et Missionariis, Bruges, 1905—
Revue du Clergé Francais, Paris, 1895-1920.

UNIVERSITAS CATHOLICA AMERICAE

WASHINGTON, D. C.

FACULTAS JURIS CANONICI

No. 74

1932

DEUS LUX MEA

TITULI

QUOS

AD DOCTORATUS GRADUM

IN

JURE CANONICO

APUD UNIVERSITATEM CATHOLICAM AMERICAE

CONSEQUENDUM

PUBLICE PROPUGNABIT

FRANCISCUS BERNARDUS DONNELLY

SACERDOS DIOECESIS BROOKLYNIENSIS

JURIS CANONICI LICENTIATUS

HORA IX A.M., DIE XX MAII MCMXXXII

TITULI

IN IURE CANONICO

I.	De Dissertatione.	
II.	De Iuris Canonici Historia.	
III.	Canones 1-7	De Ambitu Codicis.
IV.	Canones 8-24	De Legibus Ecclesiasticis.
V.	Canones 25-30	De Consuetudine.
VI.	Canones 31-35	De Temporis Supputatione.
VII.	Canones 36-62	De Rescriptis.
VIII.	Canones 118-123	De Iuribus et Privilegiis Clericorum.
IX.	Canones 492-498	De Erectione et Suppressione Religionis, Provinciae, Domus.
X.	Canones 499-517	De Superioribus et de Capitulis.
XI.	Canones 518-530	De Confessariis et de Cappellanis.
XII.	Canones 531-537	De Bonis Temporalibus Eorumque Administratione.
XIII.	Canones 539-541	De Postulatu.
XIV.	Canones 542-552	De Requisitis ut Quis in Novitiatum Admitatur.
XV.	Canones 553-571	De Novitiorum Institutione.
XVI.	Canones 572-586	De Professione Religiosa.
XVII.	Canones 587-591	De Ratione Studiorum in Religionibus Clericalibus.
XVIII.	Canones 592-612	De Obligationibus Religiosorum.
XIX.	Canones 613-625	De Privilegiis Religiosorum.
XX.	Canones 737-779	De Baptismo.
XXI.	Canones 1012-1018	De Matrimonio in Genere.
XXII.	Canones 1058-1066	De Impedimentis Impedientibus.
XXIII.	Canones 1067-1080	De Impedimentis Dirimentibus.
XXIV.	Canones 1094-1103	De Forma Celebrationis Matrimonii.
XXV.	Canones 1104-1107	De Matrimonio Conscientiae.
XXVI.	Canones 1406-1408	De Fidei Professione.
XXVII.	Canones 1552-1568	De Notione Iudicii et De Foro Competenti.
XXVIII.	Canones 1572-1593	De Tribunali Ordinario Primae Instantiae.
XXIX.	Canones 1608-1645	De Disciplina in Tribunalibus Servanda.
XXX.	Canones 1646-1666	De Partibus in Causa.
XXXI.	Canones 1706-1725	De Causae Introductione.
XXXII.	Canones 1726-1731	De Litis Instantia.
XXXIII.	Canones 1750-1753	De Confessione Partium.
XXXIV.	Canones 1770-1781	De Examine Testium.
XXXV.	Canones 1812-1824	De Probatione per Instrumenta.
XXXVI.	Canones 2162-2167	De Translatione Parochorum.
XXXVII.	Canones 2195-2198	De Natura Delicti.

XXXVIII. Canones 2214-2220 De Poenis in Genere.
XXXIX. Canones 2241-2285 De Censuris.
XL. Canones 2306-2311 De Poenalibus Remediis.
XLI. The Periods of Roman Law.
XLII. The Sources of Roman Law.
XLIII. Personality.
XLIV. Slavery.
XLV. Citizenship.
XLVI. Patria Potestas.
XLVII. Personae in Manu.
XLVIII. Tutela et Cura.
XLIX. Personae in Mancipio.
L. Ownership.
LI. De Obligationibus in Genere.
LII. De Obligationibus Extra-Contractualibus.
LIII. Furtum.
LIV. Damnum Iniuria Datum.
LV. De Actionibus.

AMERICAN CHURCH—CIVIL LAW

LVI. Juridical Status of the Church in the United States.
LVII. Methods of Holding Church Property.
LVIII. Tax Exemption.
LIX. Marriage.
LX. Cemeteries.

Vidit Facultas:

VALENTINUS T. SCHAAF, O.F.M., J.C.D., Vice-Decanus.
LUDOVICUS H. MOTRY, S.T.D., J.C.D, a Secretis.
FRANCISCUS J. LARDONE, S.T.D., J.U.D.
JOHN McDILL FOX, A.B., LL.B.

Vidit Rector Magnificus Universitatis:

JACOBUS HUGO RYAN, S.T.D., PH.D., LL.D., LITT.D.

BIOGRAPHICAL NOTE

Francis Bernard Donnelly was born in Brooklyn on June 1, 1908. After completing his elementary education in Saint Matthew's Parochial School, he entered the diocesan preparatory seminary of the Immaculate Conception and continued his classical studies there until graduation. In September, 1924, he was sent to pursue his philosophical and theological course in Saint Mary's Seminary, Baltimore, at the completion of which he came to the Catholic University for graduate work in Canon Law. He was ordained to the priesthood for the Diocese of Brooklyn on June 11, 1931.

CANON LAW STUDIES

1. FRERIKS, REV. CELESTINE A., C.PP.S., J.C.D., Religious Congregations in Their External Relations, 121 pp., 1916.
2. GALLIHER, REV. DANIEL M., O.P., J.C.D., Canonical Elections, 117 pp., 1917.
3. BORKOWSKI, REV. AURELIUS L., O.F.M., De Confraternitatibus Ecclesiasticis, 136 pp., 1918.
4. CASTILLO, REV. CAYO, J.C.D., Disertacion Historico-canonica sobre la Potestad del Cabildo en Sede Vacante o Impedida del Vicario Capitular, 99 pp., 1919 (1918).
5. KUBELBECK, REV. WILLIAM J., S.T.B., J.C.D., The Sacred Penitentiaria and Its Relations to Faculties of Ordinaries and Priests, 129 pp., 1918.
6. PETROVITS, REV. JOSEPH J. C., S.T.D., J.C.D., The New Church Law on Matrimony, X-461 pp., 1919.
7. HICKEY, REV. JOHN J., S.T.B., J.C.D., Irregularities and Simple Impediments in the New Code of Canon Law, 100 pp., 1920.
8. KLEKOTKA, REV. PETER J., S.T.B., J.C.D., Diocesan Consultors, 179 pp., 1920.
9. WANNENMACHER, REV. FRANCIS, J.C.D., The Evidence in Ecclesiastical Procedure Affecting the Marriage Bond, 1920. (Not Printed.)
10. GOLDEN, REV. HENRY FRANCIS, J.C.D., Parochial Benefices in the New Code, IV-119 pp., 1921. (Printed 1925.)
11. KOUDELKA, REV. CHARLES J., J.C.D., Pastors, Their Rights and Duties According to the New Code of Canon Law, 211 pp., 1921.
12. MELO, REV. ANTONIUS, O.F.M., J.C.D., De Exemptione Regularium, X-188 pp., 1921.
13. SCHAAF, REV. VALENTINE THEODORE, O.F.M., S.T.B., J.C.D., The Cloister, X-180 pp., 1921.
14. BURKE, REV. THOMAS JOSEPH, S.T.B., J.C.D., Competence in Ecclesiastical Tribunals, IV-117 pp., 1922.
15. LEECH, REV. GEORGE LEO, J.C.D., A Comparative Study of the Constitution "Apostolicae Sedis" and the "Codex Juris Canonici," 179 pp., 1922.
16. MOTRY, REV. HUBERT LOUIS, S.T.D., J.C.D., Diocesan Faculties according to the Code of Canon Law, II-167 pp., 1922.
17. MURPHY, REV. GEORGE LAWRENCE, J.C.D., Delinquencies and Penalties in the Administration and the Reception of the Sacraments, IV-121 pp., 1923.
18. O'REILLY, REV. JOHN ANTHONY, S.T.B., J.C.D., Ecclesiastical Sepulture in the New Code of Canon Law, II-129 pp., 1923.
19. MICHALICKA, REV. WENCESLAS CYRILL, O.S.B., J.C.D., Judicial Procedure in Dismissal of Clerical Exempt Religious, 107 pp., 1923.
20. DARGIN, REV. EDWARD VINCENT, S.T.B., J.C.D., Reserved Cases According to the Code of Canon Law, IV-103 pp., 1924.
21. GODFREY, REV. JOHN A., S.T.B., J.C.D., The Right of Patronage According to the Code of Canon Law, 153 pp., 1924.
22. HAGEDORN, REV. FRANCIS EDWARD, J.C.D., General Legislation on Indulgences, II-154 pp., 1924.

23. King, Rev. James Ignatius, J.C.D., The Administration of the Sacraments to Dying Non-Catholics, V-141 pp., 1924.
24. Winslow, Rev. Francis Joseph, A.F.M., J.C.D., Vicars and Prefects Apostolic, IV-149 pp., 1924.
25. Correa, Rev. Jose Servelion, S.T.L., J.C.D., La Potestad Legislativa de la Iglesia Católica, IV-127 pp., 1925.
26. Dugan, Rev. Henry Francis, M.A., J.C.D., The Judiciary Department of the Diocesan Curia, 87 pp., 1925.
27. Keller, Rev. Charles Frederick, S.T.B., J.C.D., Mass Stipends, 167 pp., 1925.
28. Paschang, Rev. John Linus, J.C.D., The Sacramentals According to the Code of Canon Law, 129 pp., 1925.
29. Piontek, Rev. Cyrillus, O.F.M., S.T.B., J.C.D., De Indulto Exclaustrationis necnon Saecularizationis, XIII-289 pp., 1925.
30. Kearney, Rev. Richard Joseph, S.T.B., J.C.D., Sponsors at Baptism According to the Code of Canon Law, IV-127 pp., 1925.
31. Bartlett, Rev. Chester Joseph, A.M., LL.B., J.C.D., The Tenure of Parochial Property in the United States of America, V-108 pp., 1926.
32. Kilker, Rev. Adrian Jerome, J.C.D., Extreme Unction, V-425 pp., 1926.
33. McCormick, Rev. Robert Emmett, J.C.D., Confessors of Religious, VIII-266 pp., 1926.
34. Miller, Rev. Newton Thomas, J.C.D., Founded Masses According to the Code of Canon Law, VII-93 pp., 1926.
35. Roelker, Rev. Edward G., S.T.D., J.C.D., Principles of Privilege According to the Code of Canon Law, XI-166 pp., 1926.
36. Bakalarczyk, Rev. Richardus, M.I.C., J.U.D., De Novitiatu, VIII-208 pp., 1927.
37. Pizzuti, Rev. Lawrence, O.F.M., J.U.L., De Parochis Religiosis, 1927. (Not Printed.)
38. Bliley, Rev. Nicholas Martin, O.S.B., J.C.D., Altars According to the Code of Canon Law, XIX-132 pp., 1927.
39. Brown, Brendan Francis, A.B., LL.M., J.U.D., The Canonical Juristic Personality with Special Reference to its Status in the United States of America, V-212 pp., 1927.
40. Cavanaugh, Rev. William Thomas. C.P., J.U.D., The Reservation of the Blessed Sacrament, VIII-101 pp., 1927.
41. Doheny, Rev. William J., C.S.C., A.B., J.U.D., Church Property: Modes of Acquisition, X-118 pp., 1927.
42. Feldhaus, Rev. Aloysius H., C.PP.S., J.C.D., Oratories, IX-141 pp., 1927.
43. Kelly, Rev. James Patrick, A.B., J.C.D., The Jurisdiction of the Simple Confessor, X-208 pp., 1927.
44. Neuberger, Rev. Nicholas J., J.C.D., Canon 6 or the Relation of the Codex Juris Canonici to the Preceding Legislation, V-95 pp., 1927.
45. O'Keeffe, Rev. Gerald Michael, J.C.D., Matrimonial Dispensations, Powers of Bishops, Priests, and Confessors, VIII-232 pp., 1927.
46. Quigley, Rev. Joseph, A.M., A.B., J.C.D., Condemned Societies, 139 pp., 1927.
47. Zaplotnik, Rev. Ioannes Leo, J.C.D., De Vicariis Foraneis, X-142 pp., 1927.

48. Duskie, Rev. John Aloysius, A.B., J.C.D., The Canonical Status of the Orientals in the United States, VIII-196 pp., 1928.
49. Hyland, Rev. Francis Edward, J.C.D., Excommunication, Its Nature, Historical Development and Effects, VIII-181 pp., 1928.
50. Reinmann, Rev. Gerald Joseph, O.M.C., J.C.D., The Third Order Secular of Saint Francis, 201 pp., 1928.
51. Schenk, Rev. Francis J., J.C.D., The Matrimonial Impediments of Mixed Religion and Disparity of Cult, XVI-318 pp., 1929.
52. Coady, Rev. John Joseph, S.T.D., J.U.D., A.M., The Appointment of Pastors, VIII-150 pp., 1929.
53. Kay, Rev. Thomas Henry, J.C.D., Competence in Matrimonial Procedure, VIII-164 pp., 1929.
54. Turner, Rev. Sidney Joseph, C.P., J.U.D., The Vow of Poverty, XLIX-217 pp., 1929.
55. Kearney, Rev. Raymond A., A.B., S.T.D., J.C.D., The Principles of Delegation, VII-149 pp., 1929.
56. Conran, Rev. Edward James, A.B., J.C.D., The Interdict, V-163 pp., 1930.
57. O'Neil, Rev. William H., J.C.D., Papal Rescripts of Favor, VII-218 pp.,
58. Bastnagel, Rev. Clement Vincent, J.U.D., The Appointment of Parochial Adjutants and Assistants, XV-257 pp., 1930.
59. Ferry, Rev. William A., A.B., J.C.D., Stole Fees, X-107 pp., 1930.
60. Costello, Rev. John Michael, A.B., J.C.D., Domicile and Quasi-Domicile, VII-201 pp., 1930.
61. Kremer, Rev. Michael Nicholas, A.B., S.T.B., J.C.D., Church Support in the United States, VI-136 pp., 1930.
62. Angulo, Rev. Luis, C.M., J.C.D., Legislación de la Iglesia sobre la intención en la aplicación de la Santa Misa, VII-104 pp., 1931.
63. Frey, Rev. Wolfgang Norbert, O.S.B., A.B., J.C.D., The Act of Religious Profession, VIII-174 pp., 1931.
64. Roberts, Rev. James Brendan, A.B., J.C.D., The Banns of Marriage, XIV-140 pp., 1931.
65. Ryder, Rev. Raymond Aloysius, A.B., J.C.D., Simony, IX-151 pp., 1931.
66. Campagna, Rev. Angelo, Ph.D., J.U.D., Il Vicario Generale del Vescovo, VII-205 pp., 1931.
67. Cox, Rev. Joseph Godfrey, A.B., J.C.D., The Administration of Seminaries, VI-124 pp., 1931.
68. Gregory, Rev. Donald J., J.U.D., The Pauline Privilege, XV-165 pp., 1931.
60. Donohue, Rev. John F., J.C.D., The Impediment of Crime, VIII-110 pp., 1931.
70. Dooley, Rev. Eugene A., O.M.I., J.C.D., Church Law on Sacred Relics, IX-143 pp., 1931.
71. Orth, Rev. Clement Raymond, O.M.C., J.C.D., The Approbation of Religious Institutes, 171 pp., 1931.
72. Pernicone, Rev. Joseph M., A.B., J.C.D., The Ecclesiastical Prohibition of Books, XII-267 pp., 1932.
73. Clinton, Rev. Connell, A.B., J.C.L., The Paschal Precept, 1932.
74. Donnelly, Rev. Francis B., A.M., S.T.L., J.C.L., The Diocesan Synod, 1932.

75. Torrente, Rev. Camilo, C.M.F., J.C.L., Las Processiones Sagradas, 1932.
76. Murphy, Rev. Edwin J., C.PP.S., J.C.L., Suspension Ex Informata Conscientia, 1932.
77. MacKenzie, Rev. Eric F., A.M., S.T.L., J.C.L., The Delict of Heresy in its Commission, Penalization, Absolution, 1932.
78. Lyons, Rev. Avitus E., S.T.B., J.C.L., The Collegiate Tribunal of First Instance, 1932.
79. Connolly, Rev. Thomas A., J.C.L., Appeals, 1932.
80. Sangmeister, Rev. Joseph V., A.B., J.C.L., Force and Fear as Precluding Matrimonial Consent, 1932.
81. Jaeger, Rev. Leo A., A.B., J.C.L., The Administration of Vacant and Quasi-Vacant Episcopal Sees in the United States, 1932.
82. Rimlinger, Rev. Herbert T., J.C.L., Error Invalidating Matrimonial Consent, 1932.
83. Barrett, Rev. John D. M., S.S., J.C.L., Comparative Study of the Third Plenary Council and the Code, 1932.

www.ingramcontent.com/pod-product-compliance
Lightning Source LLC
LaVergne TN
LVHW050215080826
844660LV00012B/413
9780813222639